Teacher Certification Exam

Social Science
High School

Written By:

Jeanne Ar...

n prose format

To Order Additional Copies:
Xam, Inc.
99 Central St.
Worcester, MA 01605
Toll Free   1-800-301-4647
Phone: 1-508 363 0633
Email: winwin1111@aol.
Web   www.xamonline.c
EFax   1-501-325-0185
Fax: 1-508-363-0634

XAM, INC.
Building Better Teachers

"And, while there's no reason yet to panic, I think it's only prudent that we make preperations to panic."

MTTC: Social Science High School
ISBN: 1-58197-208-3

BIOGRAPHICAL INFORMATION
JEANINE ARMESTEAD

Bachelor of Arts degree in History-Education with minor in Social Studies received from Georgia State College for Women at Milledgeville, Georgia

Thirty-two years public school teaching experience in Georgia, Texas, and Florida having taught in grades 6 - 12

Certification in: Social Studies 7 - 12; Middle School 6 - 8; Gifted K - 12; ESOL

Social Studies Department Chairperson for 16 years

Who's Who Among America's Teachers 1992 and 1994

DEDICATION:

To my many dear friends and my very large, extensive "family" who showed great patience and understanding during the work on this project and who were so encouraging in my decision to write this study guide. Special thanks and deep appreciation to the Vermeulens - Brad and Angela who unselfishly loaned the use of their computer and discs and lovingly helped me understand and learn how to use it. My love to all of you.

J.

SOCIAL SCIENCE HIGH SCHOOL

COMPETENCY 1.0 SOCIAL SCIENCES

Skill 1.1   **Be able to describe each of the social science disciplines and explain each one's methods of study and tools for research**

The disciplines within the social sciences, sometimes referred to as social studies, include anthropology, geography, history, sociology, economics, and political science. Some programs include psychology, archaeology, philosophy, religion, law, and criminology. Also, the subjects of civics and government may be a part of an educational curriculum as separate from political science.

ANTHROPOLOGY ▪ is the scientific study of human culture and humanity, the relationship between man and his culture. Anthropologists study different groups, how they relate to other cultures, patterns of behavior, similarities and differences. Their research is two-fold: cross-cultural and comparative. The major method of study is referred to as "participant observation." The anthropologist studies and learns about the people being studied by living among them and participating with them in their daily lives. Other methods may be used but this is the most characteristic method used.

ARCHAEOLOGY ▪ is the scientific study of past human cultures by studying the remains they left behind--objects such as pottery, bones, buildings, tools, and artwork. Archaeologists locate and examine any evidence to help explain the way people lived in past times. They use special equipment and techniques to gather the evidence and make special effort to keep detailed records of their findings because a lot of their research results in destruction of the remains being studied. The first step is to locate an archaeological site using various methods. Next, surveying the site takes place starting with a detailed description of the site with notes, maps, photographs, and collecting artifacts from the surface. Excavating follows, either by digging for buried objects or by diving and working in submersible decompression chambers, when underwater. They record and preserve the evidence for eventual classification, dating, and evaluating their find.

CIVICS ▪ is the study of the responsibilities and rights of citizens with emphasis on such subjects as freedom, democracy, and individual rights. Students study local, state, national, and international government structures, functions, and problems. Related to this are other social, political, and economic institutions. As a method of study, students gain experience and understanding through direct participation in student government, school publications, and other organizations. They also participate in community activities such as conservation projects and voter registration drives.

ECONOMICS ▪ generally is the study of the ways goods and services are produced and the ways they are distributed. It also includes the ways people and nations choose what they buy from what they want. Some of the methods of study include research, case studies, analysis, statistics, and mathematics.

GEOGRAPHY ▪ involves studying location and how living things and earth's features are distributed throughout the earth. It includes where animals, people, and plants live and the effects of their relationship with earth's physical features. Geographers also explore the locations of earth's features, how they got there, and why it is so important.

What geographers study can be broken down into four areas:

(1)   Location: Being able to find the exact site of anything on the earth

(2)   Spatial relations: The relationships of earth's features, places, and groups of people with one another due to their location

(3)   Regional characteristics: Characteristics of a place such as landform and climate, types of plants and animals, kinds of people who live there, and how they use the land

(4)   Forces that change the earth: Such as human activities and natural forces

Geographical studies are divided into:

(1)   Regional: Elements and characteristics of a place or region

(2)   Topical: One earth feature or one human activity occurring throughout the entire world

(3)   Physical: Earth's physical features, what creates and changes them, their relationships to each other as well as human activities

(4)   Human: Human activity patterns and how they relate to the environment, including political, cultural, historical, urban, and social geographical fields of study.

Special research methods used by geographers include mapping, interviewing, field studies, mathematics and statistics, and scientific instruments.

HISTORY ▪ is the study of the past, especially the aspects of the human past, political and economic events as well as cultural and social conditions. Students study history through textbooks, research, field trips to museums and historical sights, and other methods. Most nations set the requirement in history to study the country's heritage, usually to develop an awareness and feeling of loyalty and patriotism. History is generally divided into the three main divisions based on **(a) time periods, (b) nations, and (c) specialized topics**. Study is accomplished through research, reading, and writing about it.

POLITICAL SCIENCE ■ is the study of political life, different forms of government including elections, political parties, and public administration. Also political science studies include values such as justice, freedom, power, and equality. There are six main fields of political study in the United States:

(1) Political theory and philosophy
(2) Comparative governments
(3) International relations
(4) Political behavior
(5) Public administration
(6) American government and politics

PSYCHOLOGY ■ involves scientifically studying behavior and mental processes. The ways people and animals relate to each other are observed and recorded. Psychologists scrutinize specific patterns which will enable them to discern and predict certain behaviors, using scientific methods to verify their ideas. In this way they have been able to learn how to help people fulfill their individual human potential and strengthen understanding between individuals as well as groups and in nations and cultures. The results of the research of psychologists have deepened our understanding of the reasons for people's behavior.

Psychology is not only closely connected to the natural science of biology and the medical field of psychiatry but it is also connected to the social science areas of anthropology and sociology which have to do with people in society. Along with the sociologists and anthropologists, psychologists also study humans in their social settings, analyzing their attitudes and relationships. The disciplines of anthropology psychology, and sociology often research the same kinds of problems but from different points of view, with the emphasis in psychology on individual behavior, how an individual's actions are influenced by feelings and beliefs.

In their research, psychologists develop hypotheses, then test them using the scientific method. These methods used in psychological research include:

(1) **naturalistic observation** which includes observing the behavior of animals and humans in their natural surroundings or environment

(2) **systematic assessment** which describes assorted ways to measure the feelings, thoughts, and personality traits of people using case histories, public opinion polls or surveys, and standardized tests. These three types of assessments enable psychologists to acquire information not available through naturalistic observations

(3) **experimentation** enables psychologists to find and corroborate the cause-and-effect relationships in behavior, usually by randomly dividing the subjects into two groups: experimental group and control group

SOCIOLOGY ▪ is the study of human society: the individuals, groups, and institutions making up human society. It includes every feature of human social conditions. It deals with the predominant behaviors, attitudes, and types of relationships within a society, which is defined as a group of people with a similar cultural background living in a

specific geographical area. Sociology is divided into five major areas of study:

(1) Population studies: General social patterns of groups of people living in a certain geographical area

(2) Social behaviors: Such as changes in attitudes, morale, leadership, conformity, and others

(3) Social institutions: Organized groups of people performing specific functions within a society such as churches, schools, hospitals, business organizations, and governments

(4) Cultural influences: Including customs, knowledge, arts, religious beliefs, and language

(5) Social change: Such as wars, revolutions, inventions, fashions, and any other events or activities

Sociologists use three major methods to test and verify theories:

(1) Surveys

(2) Controlled experiments

(3) Field observation.

1.2 Be able to identify the major contributors to the study of each discipline and what their contributions are

ANTHROPOLOGY

Margaret Mead ▪ In the 1920s Margaret Mead lived among the Samoans, observing their ways of life, resulting in the book "Coming of Age in Samoa."

The Leakey family ▪ Louis, his wife Mary, and son Richard, all of whom did much field work to further the study of human origins.

ARCHAEOLOGY

Heinrich Schliemann ▪ In 1870 began excavating the site of ancient Troy in present-day Turkey.

Sir Arthur Evans ▪ In 1900 began excavating Knossos which was located on the island of Crete and which was the capital of the ancient Minoan civilization.

Howard Carter ▪ In 1922 discovered King Tutankhamen's tomb in Egypt's Valley of the Kings.

Willard F. Libby ▪ An American chemist who, in the 1940s, developed the process of radiocarbon dating.

ECONOMICS

Adam Smith ▪ Considered the "father of modern economics" whose 1776 book, "The Wealth of Nations," contained ideas still accepted by economists as the foundation or basis of free enterprise. Smith believed that economic growth resulted from free trade and free competition. He felt that government's major role in economic life was to assure effective competition.

Thomas Robert Malthus ▪ Challenged some of the ideas put forth by Adam Smith and warned that continued population growth would seriously affect, in the future, nations' ability to produce enough food for their people.

John Stuart Mill ▪ Put forth the proposal of a more equal division of profits among employers and workers.

Karl Marx and Friedrich Engels ▪ Disagreed with the idea of competition leading to economic progress and declared that free enterprise would only lead to the increase of severe depression and finally revolution by workers. In their writing, "Communist Manifesto", workers were urged to rebel against their employers and they urged for an economy of government ownership of all property.

John Maynard Keynes ▪ Wrote "The General Theory of Employment, Interest, and Money" in which he urged governments to increase their own spending in an effort to help end depressions, and he disagreed with the idea that free markets result in prosperity and full employment.

Milton Friedman ▪ An American economist who became the leading spokesman for a group of economists called "monetarists." These individuals rejected Keynes' theories and urged governments to stabilize prices and promote economic growth by raising the money supply at a constant rate.

GEOGRAPHY

Eratosthenes ▪ Ancient Greek mathematician who calculated the circumference of the earth.

Strabo ▪ Wrote a geography of the known ancient world in 17 volumes.

Ptolemy ▪ Contributed to geographic knowledge his skills in mapping and theories from studies in astronomy.

Christopher Columbus ▪ His famous first voyage sailing west to find the riches of the east and finding the Western Hemisphere instead.

Marco Polo, Vasco da Gama, and Magellan ▪ Three of many numerous explorers and colonizers who contributed to geographic knowledge.

National Geographic Society ▪ Publisher of the National Geographic magazine and the funding of expeditions and other activities furthering geographic education.

Ellen Churchill Semple and Carl Sauer ▪ U.S. geographers in the 1920s who contributed to geographical studies with emphasis on influence of environment on human history and the different ways physical surroundings are arranged by peoples of different cultures.

HISTORY

Herodotus ▪ First major Greek historian who wrote the account of the wars between the Greeks and Persians; often called the "Father of History".

Thucydides ▪ Wrote an authentic account of the war between Athens and Sparta titled "History of the Peloponnesian War".

Livy ▪ A Roman historian who wrote "History from the Founding of the City".

Eusebius ▪ Wrote "Ecclesiastical History", a history of Christianity showing God's control of human events.

Bede ▪ The Middle Ages' greatest historian who wrote "Ecclesiastical History of the English Nation" (731 A.D.), still considered the principal source for English history up to that time.

Ibn Khaldun ▪ A great Arab historian who wrote a seven-volume study of world civilization entitled "Universal History".

Edward Gibbon ▪ A British scholar who wrote the masterpiece "History of the Decline and Fall of the Roman Empire" which showed bias against Christianity and blamed Christianity partly for the fall of the Roman Empire.

Leopold von Ranke ▪ Considered the "Father of Modern History" who conceived the basic methods modern historians use to analyze and evaluate historical documents and introduced seminars to train future historians in how to do research.

POLITICAL SCIENCE

Aristotle and Plato ▪ Greek philosophers who believed that political order was to be the result of political science and that this political order would ensure maximum justice while at the same time remaining totally stable.

Saint Thomas Aquinas ▪ Elaborated further on Aristotle's theories and adapted them to Christianity, emphasizing certain duties and rights of individuals in the governmental processes. He also laid emphasis on government rule according to those rights and duties. Aquinas helped lay the foundation of the idea of modern constitutionalism by stating that government was limited by law.

Nicolo Machiavelli ▪ The famous politician from Florence who disregarded the ideals of Christianity in favor of realistic power politics.

Thomas Hobbes ▪ Whose most famous work was "Leviathan" believed that a person's life was a constant unceasing search for power and believed in the state's supremacy to combat this.

John Locke ▪ One of the most influential political writers of the 17th century who put great emphasis on human rights and put forth the belief that when governments violate those rights, people should rebel. He wrote the book "Two Treatises of Government" in 1690 which had tremendous influence on political thought in the American colonies and helped shaped the U.S. Constitution and Declaration of Independence.

Montesquieu and Rousseau ▪ Were proponents of "liberalism", the willingness to change ideas, policies, and proposals to solve current problems. They also believed that individual freedom was just as important as any community's welfare. In his work of 1762, "The Social Contract", Rousseau also described the "general will" leading to Socialism.

David Hume and Jeremy Bentham ▪ Believed that "the greatest happiness of the greatest number was the goal of politics".

John Stuart Mill ▪ Wrote extensively of the liberal ideas of his time.

Johann Gottlieb Fichte and Friedrich Hegel ▪ Three well-known German philosophers contributed significantly in the 18th century. Johann Gottlieb Fichte and Friedrich Hegel supported a liberalism which included ideas about nationalism and socialism. Immanuel Kant's liberalism included the idea of universal peace through world organization.

PSYCHOLOGY

Aristotle ▪ The Greek philosopher often credited with the beginnings of psychology. He was mainly interested in the human mind's accomplishments. He believed that the body was separate from the mind or soul which the Greeks referred to as the "psyche". He believed that the highest human virtues came from the psyche which helped people to reason.

Rene Descartes ▪ Was a French philosopher who described the strong influence of the body and mind on each other because of their being separate and suggested that the pineal gland in the brain was where this interaction took place. He developed the doctrine of "nativism", the belief that people were born able to think and reason.

Thomas Hobbes, John Locke, David Hume, and George Berkeley ▪ These men were called "empiricists", a name given to those who rejected Descartes' doctrine of nativism. These four men believed that at birth a person's mind is empty, that one gains knowledge of the outside world through the senses, and that people get ideas from their life's experiences.

Johannes P. Muller and Hermann L.F. von Hemholtz ▪ These two German scientists pioneered the first organized studies of perception and sensation, showing the feasibility of the scientific study of the physical processes that support mental activity.

William James ▪ Started what became the first psychology laboratory in the world.

William Wundt ▪ Was a German philosopher trained in physiology and medicine published the first journal dealing with experimental psychology.

It should be noted that the work of **Wundt and James** put psychology in a field by itself, separate from philosophy. Their work, along with others, led to the method of research called "introspection," training their subjects to observe and as accurately as possible record their feelings, experiences, and mental processes.

John B. Watson ▪ An American psychologist who introduced the research technique of "behaviorism", the belief that the only reliable source of information was observable behavior, not inner experiences.

Ivan Pavlov and B.F. Skinner ▪ Made significant contributions to this school of behaviorism, a reaction to the emphasis on introspection. The behaviorists believed that the environment was the important influence on one's behavior and looked for any correlation between environmental stimuli and observable behavior.

Max Wertheimer ▪ Started the school of Gestalt psychology. The word "Gestalt" is German and means a shape, pattern, or form. The proponents of this form of research studied behavior, not as different incidents of response to stimuli but as an organized pattern.

Sigmund Freud ▪ Was an Austrian physician who founded the school of psychoanalysis, the theory that repressed inner forces buried in the subconscious determined behavior and that these repressed feelings possibly affected personality problems, self-destructive behavior, and possibly physical symptoms. Freud developed a number of techniques to treat repression, including free association.

The practice of modern psychology includes the teachings of the earlier schools as well as the development of additional ones such as stimulus-response, cognitive, and humanistic psychology.

SOCIOLOGY

Auguste Comte ▪ the French philosopher who coined the term "sociology" and developed the theory called "positivism," which stated that social behavior and events could be measured scientifically.

Karl Marx and Friedrich Engels ▪ supported the theory of "economic determinism" which stated that all social patterns and institutions were controlled by economic factors which formed much of the basis of Communism.

Herbert Spencer ▪ stated that human society's development was a process occurring gradually, evolving from lower to higher forms, very much like biological evolution.

Emile Durkheim ▪ the French sociologist who was one of the first to use scientific research methods.

Max Weber ▪ Stated that sociological theories are probably generalizations.

1.3   Be able to show knowledge and understanding of concepts, vocabulary, and the interrelationships of the disciplines.

The major disciplines within the social sciences are definitely intertwined and interrelated. Knowledge and expertise in one requires background that involves some or most of the others.

Anthropology is the field of study of human culture--how different groups of people live, how they have adapted to their physical environment, what they make or produce, their relationship to other cultures, behavior, differences and similarities. To pursue the study of people, the anthropologist must know the history of the people being studied; their geography--physical environment; their governmental structure, organization, and its impact on the people; sociology is closely related to this field so knowledge and study in this area is helpful; their goods and produce and how they are used tie in with a background of economics.

Archaeology studies human cultures in the past, examining artifacts left behind to determine how certain people or groups lived their daily lives. Certainly a knowledge of history gives a background as a foundation of study. Geography makes its contribution by not only knowing where to look for remains but also how geographic conditions contributed to and affected the people or cultural groups being studied; how physical factors contributed to artifacts left behind.

Civics deals with what is required and expected of a region's citizens, their rights and responsibilities to government and each other. A knowledge of history gives the background and foundation and government or political science explains not only the organization and set-up of the government but also the impact of international relations on the country or area.

Economics is tied in mainly with history, geography, and political science. The different interrelationships include: History of economic theory and principles combined with historical background of areas; economic activities in the different countries, regions of the world and how international trade and relations are affected which leads to political science or government--how political organization and government affect an area's economic activities.

Geography is the study of the earth, its people, and how people adapt to life on earth and how they use its resources. It is undeniably connected to history, economics, political science, sociology, anthropology, and even a bit of archaeology. Geography not only deals with people and the earth today but also with:

> ► How did it all begin?
> ► What is the background of the people of an area?
> ► What kind of government or political system do they have?

► How does that affect their ways of producing goods and the distribution of them?

► What kind of relationships do these people have with other groups?

► How is the way they live their lives affected by their physical environment?

► In what ways do they effect change in their way of living?

All of this is tied in with their physical environment, the earth and its people.

History is without doubt an integral part of every other discipline in the social sciences. Knowing historical background on anything and anyone anywhere goes a long way towards explaining that what happened in the past leads up to and explains the present.

Political Science is the study of government, international relations, political thought and activity, and comparison of governments. It is tied in with history (historical background), anthropology (how government affects a group's culture and relationship with other groups), economics (governmental influence and regulation of producing and distributing goods and products), and sociology (insight into how social developments affect political life). Other disciplines are also affected as the study of political science is crucial to the understanding of the political processes and the influence of government and civic duties and responsibilities on people.

Psychology is defined as scientifically studying mental processes and behavior. It is related to anthropology and sociology, two social sciences that also study people in society. All three consider closely relationships and attitudes of humans within their social settings. Anthropology considers humans within their cultures, how they live, what they make or produce, how different groups or cultures relate to each other. Sociology follows the angle of looking at behaviors, attitudes, conditions, and relationships in human society. Psychology focuses in on individual behavior and how actions are influenced by feelings and beliefs.

Sociology studies human society with its attitudes, behaviors, conditions, and relationships with others. It is closely related to anthropology, especially applied to groups outside of one's region, nation, or hemisphere. History puts it in perspective with an historical background. Political Science is tied to sociology with the impact of political and governmental regulation of activities. Awareness of, influence of, and use of the physical environment as studied in geography also contributes to understanding. Economic activities are a part of human society. Also related would be psychology.

2.0 GEOGRAPHY

2.1 Know the earth's physical features and be able to give examples and their locations

The earth's surface is made up of 70% water and 30% land. Physical features of the land surface include mountains, hills, plateaus, valleys, and plains. Other minor landforms include deserts, deltas, canyons, mesas, basins, foothills, marshes and swamps. Earth's water features include oceans, seas, lakes, rivers, and canals.

Mountains are landforms with rather steep slopes at least 2,000 feet or more above sea level. Mountains are found in groups called mountain chains or mountain ranges. At least one range can be found on six of the earth's seven continents. North America has the Appalachian and Rocky Mountains; South America the Andes; Asia the Himalayas; Australia the Great Dividing Range; Europe the Alps; and Africa the Atlas, Ahaggar, and Drakensburg Mountains.

Hills are elevated landforms rising to an elevation of about 500 to 2000 feet. They are found everywhere on earth including Antarctica where they are covered by ice.

Plateaus are elevated landforms usually level on top. Depending on location, they range from being an area that is very cold to one that is cool and healthful. Some are dry because of being surrounded by mountains that keep out any moisture. Some examples include the Kenya Plateau in East Africa which is very cool. The plateau extending north from the Himalayas are extremely dry while those in Antarctica and Greenland are covered with ice and snow.

Plains are described as areas of flat or slightly rolling land, usually lower than the landforms next to them. Sometimes called lowlands (and sometimes located along seacoasts) they support the majority of the world's people. Some are found inland and many have been formed by large rivers. This resulted in extremely fertile soil for successful cultivation of crops and numerous large settlements of people. In North America, the vast plains areas extend from the Gulf of Mexico north to the Arctic Ocean and between the Appalachian and Rocky Mountains. In Europe rich plains extend east from Great Britain into central Europe on into the Siberian region of Russia. Plains in river valleys are found in China (the Yangtze River valley), India (the Ganges River valley), and Southeast Asia (the Mekong River valley).

Valleys are land areas that are found between hills and mountains. Some have gentle slopes containing trees and plants; others have very steep walls and are referred to as canyons. One famous example is Arizona's Grand Canyon of the Colorado River.

Deserts are large dry areas of land receiving 10 inches or less of rainfall each year. Among the more well-known deserts are Africa's large Sahara Desert, the Arabian Desert on the Arabian Peninsula, and the desert Outback covering roughly one third of Australia.

Deltas are areas of lowlands formed by soil and sediment deposited at the mouths of rivers. The soil is generally very fertile and most fertile river deltas are important crop-growing areas. One well-known example if the delta of Egypt's Nile River, known for its production of cotton.

Mesas are the flat tops of hills or mountains usually with steep sides. Sometimes plateaus are also called mesas. Basins are considered to be low areas drained by

rivers or low spots in mountains. Foothills are generally considered a low series of hills found between a plain and a mountain range. Marshes and swamps are wet lowlands providing growth of such plants as rushes and reeds.

Oceans are the largest bodies of water on the planet. The four oceans of the earth are the Atlantic Ocean, one-half the size of the Pacific and separating North and South America from Africa and Europe; the Pacific Ocean, covering almost one-third of the entire surface of the earth and separating North and South America from Asia and Australia; the Indian Ocean, touching Africa, Asia, and Australia; and the ice-filled Arctic Ocean, extending from North America and Europe to the North Pole. The waters of the Atlantic, Pacific, and Indian Oceans also touch the shores of Antarctica.

Seas are smaller than oceans and are almost completely surrounded by land. Some examples include the Mediterranean Sea found between Europe, Asia, and Africa; and the Caribbean Sea, touching the West Indies, South and Central America. A lake is a body of water completely surrounded by land. The Great Lakes in North America are a good example.

Rivers, considered a nation's lifeblood, usually begin as very small streams, formed by melting snow and rainfall, flowing from higher to lower land, emptying into a larger body of water, usually a sea or an ocean. Examples of important rivers for the people and countries affected by and/or dependent on them include the Nile, Niger, and Zaire Rivers of Africa; the Rhine, Danube, and Thames Rivers of Europe; the Yangtze, Ganges, Mekong, Hwang He, and Irrawaddy Rivers of Asia; the Murray-Darling in Australia; and the Orinoco in South America. River systams are made up of large rivers and numerous smaller rivers or tributaries flowing into them. Examples include the vast Amazon Rivers system in South America and the Mississippi River system in the United States.

Canals are man-made water passages constructed to connect two larger bodies of water. Famous examples include the Panama Canal across Panama's isthmus connecting the Atlantic and Pacific Oceans; and the Suez Canal in the Middle East between Africa and the Arabian peninsula connecting the Red Sea and Mediterranean Sea

2.2 Know the difference between climate and weather and the descriptions and locations of the different types of climates

Weather is the condition of the air which surrounds, the day-to-day atmospheric conditions including temperature, air pressure, wind and moisture or precipitation which includes rain, snow, hail or sleet.

Climate is average weather or daily weather conditions for a specific region or location over a long or extended period of time. Studying the climate of an area includes information gathered on the area's monthly and yearly temperatures and its monthly and yearly amounts of precipitation. Also a part of an area's climate is the length of its growing season. Four reasons for the different climate regions on the earth are differences in:

        (1)   Latitude
        (2)   The amount of moisture
        (3)   Tempe-ratures in land and water
        (4)   The earth's land surface.

There are many different climates throughout the earth. It is most unusual if one single country contains just one kind of climate. Regions of climates are divided according to latitudes:

        0 - 23 1/2 degrees are the "low latitudes"
        23 1/2 - 66 1/2 degrees are the "middle latitudes"
        66 1/2 degrees to the Poles are the "high latitudes"

In the **low latitudes** are the rainforest, savanna, and desert climates. The tropical rainforest climate is found in equatorial lowlands and is hot and wet. There is sun overhead, extreme heat and rain--everyday. Even though daily temperatures rarely rise above 90 degrees F., the daily humidity is always high, leaving everything sticky and damp. North and south of the tropical rainforests are located the tropical grasslands called "savannas," the "lands of two seasons"--a winter dry season and a summer wet season. Further north and south of the tropical grasslands or savannas are the deserts. These areas are the hottest and driest parts of the earth receiving less than 10 inches of rain a year. These areas have extreme temperatures between night and day. After the sun sets, the land cools quickly dropping the temperature as much as 50 degrees.

The **middle latitudes** contain the Mediterranean, humid-subtropical, humid continental, marine, steppe, and desert climates. Lands containing the Mediterranean climate are considered "sunny" lands found in six areas of the world: lands bordering the Mediterranean Sea, a small portion of southwestern Africa, areas in southern and southwestern Australia, a small part of the Ukraine near the Black Sea, central Chile, and southern California. Summers are hot and dry with mild winters. The growing season usually lasts all year and what little rain falls is usually during the winter months. What is rather unusual is that the Mediterranean climate is located between 30 and 40 degrees north and south latitude on the western coasts of countries.

The humid **subtropical climate** is found north and south of the tropics and is moist indeed. The areas having this type of climate are found on the eastern side of their continents and include Japan, mainland China, Australia, Africa, South America, and the United States--the southeastern coasts of these areas. An interesting feature of their locations is that warm ocean currents are found there. The winds that blow across these currents bring in warm moist air all year round. Long, warm summers; short, mild winters; a long growing season allowing for different crops to be grown several times a year all contribute to the productivity of this type of climate which supports more people than any of the others.

The **marine climate** is found in Western Europe, the British Isles, the U.S. Pacific Northwest, the western coast of Canada and southern Chile, along with southern New Zealand and southeastern Australia. A common characteristic of these lands are that they are either near water or surrounded by it. The ocean winds are wet and warm bringing a mild, rainy climate to these areas. In the summer, the daily temperatures average at or below 70 degrees F. During the winter, because of the warming effect of the ocean waters, the temperatures rarely fall below freezing.

In northern and central United States, northern China, south-central and southeastern Canada, and the western and southeastern parts of the former Soviet Union is found the **"climate of four seasons,"** the **humid continental climate**--spring, summer, fall, and winter. Cold winters, hot summers, and enough rainfall to grow a variety of crops are the major characteristics of this climate. In areas where the humid continental climate is found are some of the world's best farmlands as well as important activities such as trading and mining. Differences in temperatures throughout the year are determined by the distance a place is inland away from the coasts.

The **steppe or prairie climate** is located in the interiors of the large continents like Asia and North America. These dry flatlands are far from ocean breezes and are called prairies or the Great Plains in Canada and the United States and steppes in Asia. Even though the summers are hot and the winters are cold as in the humid continental climate, the big difference is rainfall. In the steppe climate, rainfall is light and uncertain, ten to 20 inches a year mainly in spring and summer and is considered normal. Where rain is more plentiful, grass grows; in areas of less, the steppes or prairies gradually become deserts. These are found in the Gobi Desert of Asia, central and western Australia, southwestern United States, and in the smaller deserts found in Pakistan, Argentina, and Africa south of the Equator.

The two major climates found in the high latitudes are **"tundra" and "taiga."** The word "tundra" meaning "marshy plain" is a Russian word and aptly describes the climatic conditions in the northern areas of Russia, Europe, and Canada. Winters are extremely cold and very long. Most of the year the ground is frozen but becomes rather mushy during the very short summer months. Surprisingly less snow falls in the area of the tundra than in the eastern part of the United States. However, due to the harshness of the extreme cold, very few people live there and no crops can be raised. Despite having a small human population, many plants and animals are found there.

The **"taiga"** is the northern forest region and is located south of the tundra. In fact, the Russian word "taiga" means "forest." The world's largest forest lands are found here along with vast mineral wealth and furbearing animals. The climate is so extreme that very few people live here, not being able to raise crops due to the extremely short growing season. The winter temperatures are colder and the summer temperatures are hotter than those in the tundra due to the the fact that the taiga climate region is farther from the waters of the Arctic Ocean. The taiga is found in the northern parts of Russia, Sweden, Norway, Finland, Canada, and Alaska with most of their lands covered with marshes and swamps.

In certain areas of the earth exists a type of climate unique to areas with high mountains, usually different from their surroundings. This type of climate is called a **"vertical climate"** because the temperatures, crops, vegetation, and human activities change and become different as one ascends the different levels of elevation. At the foot of the mountain a hot and rainy climate is found with the cultivation of many lowland crops. As one climbs higher, the air becomes cooler, the climate changes sharply and different economic activities change, such as grazing sheep and growing corn. At the top of many mountains, snow is found all year round.

2.3   Be able to explain how physical and political locations are determined and give examples

Physical locations of the earth's surface features include the four major hemispheres and the parts of the earth's continents in them. Political locations are basically the political divisions, if any, within each continent. Both physical and political locations are precisely determined in two ways: (1) Surveying is done to determine boundary lines and distance from other features. (2) Exact locations are precisely determined by imaginary lines of **latitude** (parallels) and **longitude** (meridians). The intersection of these lines at right angles forms a grid, making it possible to pinpoint an exact location of any place using any two grip coordinates.

The **Eastern Hemisphere**, located between the North and South Poles and between the Prime Meridian (0 degrees longitude) east to the International Date Line at 180 degrees longitude, consists of most of Europe, all of Australia, most of Africa, and all of Asia, except for a tiny piece of the eastern-most part of Russia that extends east of 180 degrees longitude.

The **Western Hemisphere**, located between the North and South Poles and between the Prime Meridian (0 degrees longitude) west to the International Date Line at 180 degrees longitude, consists of all of North and South America, a tiny part of the easternmost part of Russia that extends east of 180 degrees longitude, and a part of Europe that extends west of the Prime Meridian (0 degrees longitude).

The **Northern Hemisphere**, located between the North Pole and the Equator, contains all of the continents of Europe and North America and parts of South America, Africa, and most of Asia. The **Southern Hemisphere**, located between the South Pole and the Equator, contains all of Australia, a small part of Asia, about one-third of Africa, most of South America, and all of Antarctica.

Of the **seven continents**, only one contains just one entire country and also is the only island continent, **Australia**. Its political divisions consist of six states and one territory: Western Australia, South Australia, Tasmania, Victoria, New South Wales, Queensland, and Northern Territory.

Africa is made up of 54 separate countries, the major ones being Egypt, Nigeria, South Africa, Zaire, Kenya, Algeria, Morocco, and the large island of Madagascar.

Asia consists of 49 separate countries, some of which include China, Japan, India, Turkey, Israel, Iraq, Iran, Indonesia, Jordan, Vietnam, Thailand, and the Philippines. Europe's 43 separate nations include France, Russia, Malta, Denmark, Hungary, Greece, Bosnia and Herzegovina.

North American consists of not only Canada and the United States of America but also the island nations of the West Indies and the "land bridge" of Middle America, including Cuba, Jamaica, Mexico, Panama, and others.

Thirteen separate nations together occupy the continent of **South America**, among them such nations as Brazil, Paraguay, Ecuador, and Suriname.

The continent of **Antarctica** has no political boundaries or divisions but is the location of a number of science and research stations managed by nations such as Russia, Japan, France, Australia, and India.

2.4   Be able to show an understanding of the relationship of geography to culture

Social scientists use the term **culture** to describe the way of life of a group of people. This would include not only art, music, and literature but also beliefs, customs, languages, traditions, inventions--in short, any way of life whether complex or simple. The term geography is defined as the study of earth's features and living things as to their location, relationship with each other, how they came to be there, and why so important.

Physical geography is concerned with the locations of such earth features as climate, water, and land; how these relate to and affect each other and human activities; and what forces shaped and changed them. All three of these earth features affect the lives of all humans having a direct influence on what is made and produced, where it occurs, how it occurs, and what makes it possible. The combination of the different climate conditions and types of landforms and other surface features works together all around the earth to give the many varied cultures their unique characteristics and distinctions.

Cultural geography studies the location, characteristics, and influence of the physical environment on different cultures around the earth. Also included in these studies are comparisons and influences of the many varied cultures. Ease of travel and up-to-the-minute, state-of-the-art communication techniques ease the difficulties of understanding cultural differences making it easier to come in contact with them.

3.0 ECONOMICS

3.1 Be able to apply the principles of consumer economics

A **consumer** is a person who uses goods and services and, in a **capitalist** or free enterprise economy, decides with other consumers what is produced by what they choose to buy. The terms **"supply and demand"** are used to explain the influence of consumers on production. This law or principle of supply and demand means that prices of goods rise due to an increased demand and fall when there is an increase in the supply of goods.

Due to unstable economies, inflation, job insecurity due to downsizing, bankruptcy and other factors, having cash on hand while buying is less prevalent than having a **credit card**. These are frequently referred to as "plastic money" but in reality are not money. They are a convenient tool for receiving a short-term loan from whatever financial institutions issued the cards. These popular pieces of plastic aid consumers in such economic activities as purchasing items on "installment plans." Financial institutions are not the only ones issuing credit cards. Oil companies, airlines, national automobile manufacturers, large corporations are just some of the backers of credit cards. Department store charge cards do not enable the holder to obtain money from an **ATM** but do enable one to buy on credit or on the installment plan. Automobile dealerships, banks, credit unions, loan companies all, in similar ways, make it possible for just about anyone to purchase on installment and drive a car. Mortgages allow people to pay for their own home or condominium.

3.2. Give descriptions and comparisons of various economic systems

Capitalism (or Free Enterprise)

This economic system provides for individual ownership of land and capital allowing individuals to pursue their economic activities with as little government control or interference as possible. The individuals are the consumers, owners, managers, workers, producers, and make their own economic decisions. The vast majority of the means of production are owned by individuals, not the government. This type of economic system is used and practiced in such countries as the United States and Canada. However, Canada tends to be more socialistic as exemplified by their national health care system. It is not as capitalistic as the United States.

Mixed Economies

This economic system has more control and planning by the government than in capitalist economies. The government owns and operates key industries such as the railroads, steel mills, and coal mines. Individuals are allowed to own most of the other industries. The main type of a mixed economy is "socialism". Proponents of socialism feel that the capitalistic free enterprise system is wasteful, inefficient, and leads to serious economic problems such as poverty, unemployment, cycles in business, and conflicts between management and labor. One variety of socialism favors basic industries owned by the government, private ownership of other businesses, and government regulation of privately-owned businesses. In non-Communist lands, some countries with a socialist economy provide for democratic ways to decide what goods will be produced. The people choose the government, casting votes on some of the economic policies. Sometimes they also vote on how much control over the economy the government has, increasing or reducing it whenever adjustments need to be made. This type of economic system is sometimes called "democratic socialism" and is practiced in such countries as Sweden and Great Britain.

Communism

This economic system is based on the theory that the government not only owns all productive resources but also directs all of the important economic activities, deciding what is produced, how much to produce, prices, workers' wages, and even the rate of economic growth. The only exception would be the private land plots for personal use and production. Choice of products to buy is left up to the consumers but quantity, quality, and choice are limited. The people have no control over the government's economic policies. This type of economic system is practiced in the few remaining "Communist" nations, such as China, North Korea, and Cuba.

3.3   Show an understanding of the role of markets

A "market" is an economic term to describe the places and situations in which goods and services are bought and sold. In a capitalistic free enterprise economy, the market prices of goods and services rise and fall according to decreases and increases in the supply and demand and the degree of competition.

In an economic system, there is also a "market" for land, capital, and labor. The labor market, for example, is studied by economists in order to better understand trends in jobs, productivity of workers, activities of labor unions, and patterns of employment. Potential customers for a product or service are also called a market and are the subject of market research to determine who would possibly make use of whatever is offered to customers.

Other types of markets which are parts of countries' economic systems include the following:

Stock Market

This is part of a capitalistic free enterprise system and is one of significant investment and speculation.   Any changes in the prices of stocks are seriously affected by those who buy stocks when their prices are rising and sell them when their prices are start to

fall. Business planners quite often regard the stock market as a barometer of the degree of confidence investors have in the conditions of businesses in the future. When the stock market is a rising "bull" market, economists and investors see it as the public showing confidence in the future of business. At the same time, when the market is a falling "bear" market, it is an indication of a lack of confidence. In unstable economic conditions, one or more of a number of conditions and situations can seriously affect the stock market's rise and fall. The "bottom line" is that these fluctuations are directly tied to and directly affected by investment changes.

"Black" Market

This illegal market has in the past and even today exists in countries where wage and price controls are in place and enforced by law. In these markets, goods and products are priced and sold above legal limits, especially if the maximum legal price is much less than free-market price, if certain products are unavailable in the regulated market, or if wage and price controls are in place for an extended period of time.

Common Market

This market, also called the European Economic Community (EEC), began in 1958 and is made up of several European nations. Its major purpose was to remove all restrictive tariffs and import quotas in order to encourage and facilitate free trade among member nations. Included also were efforts to move workers and services without restrictions.

3.4   Be able to understand and illustrate global economic concepts

"Globalism" is defined as the principle of the interdependence of all the world's nations and their peoples. Within this global community, every nation, in some way to a certain degree, is dependent on other nations. Since no one nation has all of the resources needed for production, trade with other nations is required to obtain what is needed for production, to sell what is   produced or to buy finished products, to earn money--in other words, to maintain and strengthen the nation's economic system.

Developing nations receive technical assistance and financial aid from developed nations. Many international organizations have been set up to promote and encourage cooperation and economic progress among member nations. Through the elimination of such barriers to trade as tariffs, trade is stimulated resulting in increased productivity, economic progress, increased cooperation and understanding on the diplomatic levels.

Those nations not part of an international trade organization not only must make those economic decisions of what to produce, how and for whom, but must also deal with the problem of tariffs and quotas on imports. Regardless of international trade memberships, economic growth and development are vital and affect all trading nations. Businesses, labor, and governments share common interests and goals in a nation's economic status. International systems of banking and finance have been devised to assist governments and businesses in setting the policy and guidelines for the exchange of currencies.

4.0 POLITICAL SCIENCE

4.1 Be able to show knowledge of the American political and governmental systems, including the national, state, and local levels

The American governmental system is a federal system--fifty individual states federated or forming or uniting as one nation. The national and state governments share the powers of government. This federal system required decentralization which makes it impossible to coexist with totalitarianism. Both national and state governments exist and govern by the will of the people who are the source of their authority. Local governmental systems operate under the same guidelines.

The American political system is a two-party system, consisting of the Democratic and Republican parties. Political parties in America have approximately five major functions:

(1)   They choose candidates who will run for public office
(2)   They assist in organizing the government
(3)   They oppose the political party in power
(4)   They obtain the funds needed to conduct election campaigns
(5)   They take the initiative to make sure voters are aware of issues, problems to be solved, and any other information about public affairs.

The two-party system in America operates at the national, state, and local levels.

4.2 Know and understand the major principles of the U.S. Constitution

The U.S. Constitution set up a federal system of government, dividing powers between the national and state governments. The national government is **balanced** by having its authority divided among the three branches.

The legislative branch includes **Congress** and eight administrative agencies. Congress is made up of the **House of Representatives and the Senate**. It is the responsibility of the U.S. Congress to make, repeal, and amend all federal laws as well as levying federal taxes and distributing funds for the government.

The **U.S. Senate** consists of 100 members, two from each state regardless of size or population, who serve six-year terms. Its exclusive powers include approval of Presidential nominations for major federal offices, approval of any treaty made, and conducting impeachment cases of federal officials. Charges for impeachment include treason, bribes, high crimes and misdemeanors. The **Vice-President** presides at all impeachment proceedings except in the case of the President, when the Chief Justice of the Supreme Court presides. Two-thirds of the Senate must agree on the verdict.

The **House of Representatives** has 435 members who serve two-year terms. The number of representatives from each state is determined by population with a guarantee of at least one representative regardless. The number of representatives is set by law and is not subject to change. Its exclusive powers include initiating all money bills and bringing impeachment charges against high federal officials.

The **executive branch** includes the Executive Office of the President, various executive departments and independent agencies. The U.S. President is the nation's chief of state, chief executive, and the head of the government of the United States. He is responsible for enforcing federal laws, appointing and removing any high federal officials, commanding all the armed forces, conducting foreign affairs, and recommending laws to Congress. He is responsible for appointing American representatives to carry out diplomatic missions in foreign lands and to serve in international organizations. The President is also required to perform many ceremonial duties. He is elected to a term of four years and is limited constitutionally to no more than two terms.

The **judicial branch** is made up of the Supreme Court and other lower federal courts. Consisting of a chief justice and eight associate justices, the Supreme Court is the highest court in the land. All nine justices are appointed by the president with Senate approval. The lower federal courts consist of district courts, courts of appeal, and a group of courts handling specialized cases. All federal courts hear cases involving the Constitution and federal laws. These judges are also appointed by the President with Senate approval and, along with the Supreme Court justices, hold office for life. Under the process called "judicial review" (as set forth in "Marbury vs Madison, 1803), the Supreme Court has the authority to declare unconstitutional any executive orders or any legislative acts of both federal and state governments, based on the statement in the U.S. Constitution stating that it and all treaties and federal laws are the supreme law of the land.

The U.S. Constitution created a federal government solidly based on four fundamental principles. The **first principle** is that of "federalism," a system of government in which powers are divided between the national and state governments. This, in turn, set up four types of governmental powers:

(1) delegated or expressed ▪ those listed directly
(2) implied powers ▪ not stated directly but suggested
(3) reserved powers ▪ not given to the national government but reserved for the people or for the states
(4) concurrent powers ▪ given to both national and state govern-ments at the same time

The **second principle** is the separation of powers with the system of checks and balances. The writers of the Constitution were greatly concerned about protecting the new nation from any form of tyranny, seizure of power by a military dictator, or any one branch of government becoming stronger and more powerful than the others. Therefore it was determined to keep the three branches separate and equal. Additionally a system of checks and balances was written into the Constitution. This gives each of the three branches some powers that affect the other two. Some examples include: Congress checks the President by having the authority to appropriate funds for running the government. Congress checks the judicial branch due to its power to provide for and set up the courts along with their rules of procedure. The President can check Congress with his power to veto bills it passes. The President checks the courts with his power to appoint judges and justices. The courts can check both Congress and the President by reviewing executive orders and legislative acts and declaring them unconstitutional.

A **third principle** provides for the protection of individual rights and liberties. These provisions include the following: The Constitution prohibits the passage of "ex post facto laws" (laws passed "after the deed" providing the penalty for an act that was not an illegal act at the time it was committed) and "bills of attainder" (laws that render punishment to someone through fines, imprisonment, and confiscation of property without a court trial first). Individual rights are also protected by granting one a "writ of habeas corpus" which is a legal document requiring release from jail or prison if an individual has not been formally charged with or convicted of a crime. Special protection is given to those accused of treason as well as their innocent relatives. The accused was entitled to a fair trial and due process of law and would be protected against being accused merely because of criticism against the government. Treason was defined by the Constitution as waging war against the United States or supporting enemies of the U.S. giving them assistance. It would require at least two witnesses testifying for conviction. Only the guilty would be convicted and punished; no punishment or penalty is allowed against that one's family or relatives.

The first ten amendments to the Constitution, known as **the Bill of Rights**, guaranteed protection for individuals against any action by the federal government which would threaten the loss of their life, liberty, or property without proper legal procedure. These laws guaranteed freedoms such as speech, press, assembly, religion, petition, unreasonable searches and seizures, and protection against arbitrary arrest and punishment.

The fourth principle is the fact that for over 200 years the Constitution has adapted to changing times and circumstances. One important process is the ability to meet needed changes through amendments. The other great reason for its flexibility is the inclusion of what is known as the "elastic clause." In addition to its specific powers, the writers granted to Congress the power to make any additional laws needed and appropriate in order to implement other powers.

The U.S. Constitution is a most unique document among human governments today. It has stood the test of time for two reasons: (1) It has set out procedural rules that must be followed, even in extreme and critical circumstances; and (2) due to amending along with customs and practices, it is flexible and adaptable making it possible to meet the demands and changes of a growing nation.

4.3 Recognize the rights and responsibilities of U.S. citizens

Citizens' rights vary from nation to nation. The U.S. Constitution and Congressional laws provide basic as well as additional rights to American citizens. These civil rights include such rights as freedom of religion, assembly, speech, voting, holding public office, and traveling throughout the country. U.S. citizens have the right to live in America and cannot be forced to leave. American citizenship is guaranteed and will not be taken away for any reason, unless one commits certain serious actions. Citizens' rights have limitations such as minimum age for voting and limited free speech, forbidding the damage to someone's reputation by slander and lying.

Citizens' duties also vary from nation to nation. Duties demanded by law (also considered civic responsibilities) include paying taxes, obeying the laws, and defending the country. Although some governments require jury duty, in the United States this would be a duty not required by law along with voting, doing volunteer work to help others, and becoming aware of public problems. Citizenship is granted one of two ways: either by birth or by naturalization. Some hold citizenship in two nations the same two ways.

4.4 Be able to recognize and understand the main features of international relations

The governments of all independent states are considered "sovereign", meaning that each national government does not recognize any authority higher than its own . Governments of all countries seek benefits for their citizens which result in cooperating

with each other if this is in the best interests of their nation. Peaceful relations between countries are maintained by four methods:

(1) Diplomacy

The day-to-day relations between governments are carried out by ambassadors and other diplomats. They arrange treaties; work to get political advantages for their government; protect the interests of their fellow citizens who are traveling abroad; and make every effort to settle any disputes through negotiations.

(2) International Conferences and Organizations

If many countries have an international problem or if several disagreements must be settled, an international conference may be convened. Some international or multi-national organizations, the United Nations for example, may become involved.

(3) Treaties

These are considered formal agreements, used by national governments for various reasons such as: providing for military protection, ending military conflict, promoting economic interests, establishing important agencies and organizations, and drawing and limiting borders.

(4) International law

This area develops and sets up, either in treaties or through custom, rules and guidelines for governments to observe in pursuing their relations with one another.

4.5 Be able to understand and to compare different political theories and systems

A political system can be explained or defined as the unique way a nation governs itself. There are several different political systems in existence:

(1) Monarchy ▪ a government ruled by a king or queen. Most monarchies are considered constitutional or limited, meaning that the king or queen does not have sole, absolute authority but that executive power is usually carried out through a prime minister and cabinet and laws are made in a legislative body, such as a parliament.

(2) Oligarchy ▪ a type of modern government in which a small group of people control the government. Some examples are a republic, an aristocracy, even some dictatorships, especially if based on wealth or military authority.

(3) Democracy ▪ means "rule by the people." There are **two types of democracy**:

(a) pure or direct democracy ▪ when the citizens themselves meet in one place and make laws for themselves and their community. A familiar example of this form was in ancient Greece practiced by the citizens of Athens.

The other type is (b) representative democracy ▪ practiced by most modern democracies. Usually it is impossible or most inconvenient for all the people to meet in one place to make laws. So they choose or elect representatives to meet and make laws for them. This form of government is also sometimes referred to as republican government or a democratic republic.

(4) Despotism and Dictatorships ▪ a form of government and any ruler where there is unlimited power over the people and no legislative body to limit rulership. This is similar to the definitions for tyranny, autocracy, and totalitarianism.

(5) Parliamentary system ▪ a government made up of a legislative body, called a parliament, and a cabinet with a premier or prime minister heading the cabinet. The cabinet is chosen and supported by the majority political party in parliament and stays in power as long as it has this support.

(6) Presidential system ▪ a government of separate executive and legislative branches. The executive branch is headed by a president, elected for a fixed term.

(7) Federalism ▪ a single government of limited powers under which two or more sovereign political units, such as states or provinces, are united.

(8) Constitutionalism ▪ a political system in which laws and traditions limit the powers of government.

5.0 WORLD HISTORY

5.1 Establish an understanding of prehistory and the ancient civilizations, including the non-Western world

Prehistory is defined as the period of man's achievements before the development of writing. In the Stone Age cultures the three different periods with their accomplishments include the Lower Paleolithic period with the use of crude tools; the Upper Paleolithic period exhibiting a greater variety of better-made tools and implements, the wearing of clothing, highly organized group life, and skills in art; and the Neolithic period which showed domesticated animals, food production, the arts of knitting, spinning and weaving cloth, starting fires through friction, building houses rather than living in caves, the development of institutions including the family, religion, and a form of government or the origin of the state.

Ancient civilizations were those cultures which developed to a greater degree and were considered advanced. These included the following eleven with their major accomplishments:

Egypt made numerous significant contributions including construction of the great pyramids; development of hieroglyphic writing; preservation of bodies after death; making paper from papyrus; contributing to developments in arithmetic and geometry; the invention of the method of counting in groups of 10 (the decimal system) but had nothing to denote or represent zero; completion of a solar calendar; and laying the foundation for science and astronomy.

The ancient civilization of the **Sumerians** invented the wheel; developed irrigation through use of canals, dikes, and devices for raising water; devised the system of cuneiform writing; learned to divide time; and built large boats for trade. The Babylonians devised the famous Code of Hammurabi, a code of laws.

The ancient **Assyrians** were warlike and aggressive due to a highly organized military and used chariots drawn by horses. The **Hebrews**/ancient Israelites instituted "monotheism," which is the worship of one God, Yahweh, and combined the 66 books of the Hebrew and Christian Greek scriptures into the Bible we have today.

The **Minoans** had a system of writing using symbols to represent syllables in words; built palaces with multiple levels containing many rooms, water and sewage systems with flush toilets, bathtubs, hot and cold running water, and bright paintings on the walls.

The **Mycenaeans** changed the Minoan writing system to aid their own language and also used symbols to represent syllables.

The **Phoenicians** were sea traders well-known for their manufacturing skills in glass and metals; the development of their famous purple dye; became so very proficient in the skill of navigation that they were able to sail by the stars at night; devised an alphabet using symbols to represent single sounds, which was an improved extension of the Egyptian principle and writing system.

In **India**, the caste system was developed, the principle of zero in mathematics was discovered, and the major religion of **Hinduism** was begun.

China began building the Great Wall; practiced crop rotation and terrace farming; increased the silk industry in importance; developed caravan routes across Central Asia for extensive trade; increased proficiency in rice cultivation; developed a written language based on drawings or pictographs (no alphabet symbolizing sounds as each word or character had a form different from all others).

The ancient **Persians** developed an alphabet; contributed the religions/philosophies of Zoroastrianism, Mithraism, and Gnosticism; allowed conquered peoples to retain their own customs, laws, and religions.

5.2 Understand the important contributions of classical civilizations, including the non-Western world

The classical civilization of **Greece** reached the highest levels in man's achievements based on the foundations already laid by such ancient groups as the Egyptians, Phoenicians, Minoans, and Mycenaeans. Among the more important contributions of Greece were: from the Phoenicians the letters for the Greek alphabet forming the basis for the Roman and our present-day alphabets; extensive trading and colonization resulting in the spread of the Greek civilization; the love of sports with emphasis on a sound body, leading to the tradition of the Olympic games; the rise of independent, strong city-states; the complete contrast between independent, freedom-loving Athens with its practice of pure democracy (direct, personal, active participation in government by qualified citizens) and rigid, totalitarian, militaristic Sparta; important accomplishments in drama, epic and lyric poetry, fables, myths centered around the many gods and goddesses, science, astronomy, medicine, mathematics, philosophy, art, architecture, writing about and recording historical events; the conquests of Alexander the Great spreading Greek ideas to the areas he conquered and bringing to the Greek world many ideas from Asia; and above all, the value of ideas, wisdom, curiosity, and the desire to learn as much about the world as was possible.

The ancient civilization of Rome lasted approximately 1,000 years including the periods of republic and empire, although its lasting influence on Europe and its history was for a much longer period of time. There was a very sharp contrast between the curious, imaginative, inquisitive Greeks and the practical, simple, down-to-earth, no-nonsense

Romans who spread and preserved the ideas of ancient Greece and other culture groups. The contributions and accomplishments of the Romans are numerous but their greatest include language, engineering and building, law, government, roads, trade, and the **"Pax Romana"** ▪ the long period of peace enabling free travel and trade, spreading people, cultures, goods, and ideas all over a vast area of the known world.

A most interesting and significant characteristic of the Greek, Hellenic, and Roman civilizations was **"secularism"** where emphasis shifted away from religion to the state. Men were not absorbed in or dominated by religion as had been the case in Egypt and the nations located in Mesopotamia. Religion and its leaders did not dominate the state and its authority was greatly diminished.

In **India Hinduism** was a continuing influence along with the rise of Buddhism. Industry and commerce developed along with extensive trading with the Near East. Outstanding advances in the fields of science and medicine were made along with being one of the first to be active in navigation and maritime enterprises during this time period.

China is considered by some historians as the oldest, uninterrupted civilization in the world and was in existence around the same time as the ancient civilizations found in Egypt, Mesopotamia, and the Indus Valley. The Chinese studied nature and weather; stressed the importance of education, family, and a strong central government; followed the religions of **Buddhism, Confucianism, and Taoism**; and invented such things as gunpowder, paper, printing, and the magnetic compass.

The civilization in **Japan** appeared in this time period having borrowed much of their culture from China. It was the last of these classical civilizations to develop and although they used, accepted, and copied Chinese art, law, architecture, dress, writing, and others, the Japanese refined these into their own unique way of life, including incorporating the religion of Buddhism into their culture.

The civilizations in **Africa** south of the Sahara were developing the refining and use of iron, expecially for farm implements and later for weapons. Trading was overland using camels and at important seaports. The Arab influence was extremely important as was their later contact with Indians, Christian Nubians, and Persians. In fact, their trading activities were probably the most important factor in the spread of and assimilation of different ideas and stimulation of cultural growth.

5.3 Show an understanding of the period known as the Middle Ages

The official end of the **Roman Empire** came when Germanic tribes took over and controlled most of Europe. The five major ones were the Visigoths, Ostrogoths, Vandals, Saxons, and the Franks. In later years, the Franks successfully stopped the invasion of southern **Europe** by Muslims by soundly defeating them, under the leadership of Charles Martel, at the Battle of Tours in 732 A.D. Thirty-six years later in 768 A.D. the grandson of Charles Martel became King of the Franks and is known in history as Charlemagne. Charlemagne was a man of war but was unique in his respect for and encouragement of learning. He made great efforts to rule fairly and ensure just treatment for his people.

The **Vikings** had a lot of influence at this time with their spreading ideas and their knowledge of trade routes and sailing, accomplished first through their conquests and later through trade.

The purpose of the Crusades was to rid Jerusalem of Muslim control and these series of violent, bloody conflicts did affect trade and stimulated later explorations seeking the new, exotic products such as silks and spices. The **Crusaders** came into contact with other religions and cultures and spread and received many new ideas.

During this time period, the system of **feudalism** became the dominant feature. It was a system of loyalty and protection. The strong protected the weak who returned the service with farm labor, military service, and loyalty. Life was lived out on a vast estate, owned by a nobleman and his family, called a "manor." It was in actuality a complete village supporting a few hundred people, mostly peasants. Improved tools and farming methods made life more bearable although most never left the manor or traveled from their village their entire lifetime.

Also coming into importance at this time were the era of **knighthood** and its code of chivalry as well as the tremendous influence of the Church (Roman Catholic). Until the period of the Renaissance, the Church was the only place where people could be educated. The Bible and other books were hand-copied by monks in the monastaries. Cathedrals were built and were decorated with art depicting religious subjects.

With the increase in trade and travel, cities sprang up and began to grow. Craftworkers in the cities developed their skills to a high degree, eventually organizing **guilds** to protect the quality of the work and to regulate the buying and selling of their products. City government developed and fluorished, centered on strong town councils. Active in city government and the town councils were the wealthy businessmen who made up the rising middle class.

The end of the **feudal manorial system** was sealed by the outbreak and spread of the infamous Black Death which killed over one-third of the total population of Europe. Those who survived and were skilled in any job or occupation were in demand and many serfs or peasants found freedom and, for that time period, a decidedly improved standard of living. Strong nation-states became powerful and people developed a renewed interest in life and learning.

In other parts of the world were the **Byzantine and Saracenic** (or Islamic) civilizations, both dominated by religion. The major contributions of the Saracens were in the areas of science and philosophy. Included were accomplishments in astronomy, mathematics, physics, chemistry, medicine, literature, art, trade and manufacturing, agriculture, and a marked influence on the Renaissance period of history.

The Byzantines (Christians) made important contributions in art and the preservation of Greek and Roman achievements including architecture (especially in eastern Europe and Russia), the Code of Justinian and Roman law.

5.4 Show an understanding of the importance and accomplishments of the Renaissance and Reformation periods

The word "Renaissance" literally means "rebirth" and signaled the rekindling of interest in the glory and learning of ancient classical Greece and Rome. It was the period of time in human history marking the start of many ideas and innovations leading to our modern age.

The **Renaissance** began in Italy with many of its ideas starting in Florence, controlled by the infamous Medici family. Education, especially for some of the merchants, required reading, writing, math, the study of law, and the writings of classical Greece and Rome. Contributions of the Italian Renaissance period were in:

(1) art ▪ the more important artists were Giotto and his development of perspective in paintings; Leonardo da Vinci who was not only an artist but also a scientist and inventor; Michelangelo who was a sculptor, painter, and architect; others included Raphael, Donatello, Titian, and Tintoretto

(2) political philosophy ▪ the writings of Machiavelli

(3) literature ▪ the writings of Petrarch and Boccaccio

(4) science ▪ Galileo

(5) medicine ▪ the work of Brussels-born Andrea Vesalius earned him the title of "father of anatomy" and had a profound influence on the Spaniard Michael Servetus and the Englishman William Harvey.

In Germany, Gutenberg's invention of the **printing press** with movable type facilitated the rapid spread of Renaissance ideas, writings and innovations, thus insuring the enlightenment of most of Western Europe. Also in Germany, contributions were made by Durer and Holbein in art and by Paracelsus in science and medicine.

The effects of the Renaissance in the Low Countries can be seen in the literature and philosophy of Erasmus and the art of van Eyck and Breughel the Elder. Rabelais and de Montaigne in France also made contributions in literature and philosophy. In Spain the art of El Greco and de Morales fluorished as did the writings of Cervantes and de Vega. In England Sir Thomas More and Sir Francis Bacon wrote and taught philosophy and inspired by Vesalius, William Harvey made important contributions in medicine. The greatest talent was found in literature and drama given to mankind by **Chaucer, Spenser, Marlowe, Jonson, and the incomparable Shakespeare.**

The **Reformation** period consisted of two phases: the Protestant Revolution and the Catholic Reformation. The Protestant Revolution came about because of religious, political, and economic reasons. The religious reasons stemmed from abuses in the Catholic Church including fraudulent clergy with their scandalous immoral lifestyles; the sale of religious offices, indulgences, and dispensations; different theologies within the Church; and frauds involving sacred relics.

The political reasons for the **Protestant Revolution** involved the increase in the power of rulers who were considered "absolute monarchs" wanting all power and control, especially over the Church; and the growth of "nationalism" or patriotic pride in one's own country.

Economic reasons included the greedy desire of ruling monarchs to possess and control all lands and wealth of the Church; deep animosity against the burdensome papal taxation; the rise of the affluent middle class and its clash with medieval Church ideals; and the increase of an active system of "intense" capitalism.

The Protestant Revolution began in Germany with the revolt of **Martin Luther** against Church abuses. It spread to Switzerland where it was led by Calvin. It began in England with the efforts of King Henry VIII to have his marriage to Catherine of Aragon annulled so he could wed another and have a male heir. The results were the increasing support given not only by the people but also by nobles and some rulers and of course the attempts of the Church to stop it.

The **Catholic Reformation** was undertaken by the Church to "clean up its act" and to slow down or stop the Protestant Revolution. The major efforts to this end were supplied by the Council of Trent and the Jesuits. Six major results of the Reformation include:

- Religious freedom
- Religious tolerance
- More opportunities for education
- Power and control of rulers limited
- Increase in religious wars
- An increase in fanaticism and persecution

5.5 Understand the importance and results of the Age of Exploration

A number of different individuals and events led to the time period of exploration and discoveries. The **Vivaldo brothers and Marco Polo** wrote of their travels and experiences which signaled the early beginnings. From the Crusades, the survivors made their way home to different places in Europe bringing with them fascinating, new information about exotic lands, people, customs, and desired foods and goods such as spices and silks.

The Renaissance ushered in a time of curiosity, learning, and incredible energy sparking the desire for trade to procure these new, exotic products and to find better, faster, cheaper trade routes to get to them. The work of geographers, astronomers and map-makers made important contributions and many studied and applied the work of such men as **Hipparchus of Greece, Ptolemy of Egypt, Tycho Brahe of Denmark, and Fra Mauro of Italy**.

Portugal made the start under the encouragement, support, and financing of Prince Henry the Navigator. The more well-known explorers who sailed under the flag of Portugal included **Cabral, Diaz, and Vasco da Gama**, who successfully sailed all the way from Portugal, around the southern tip of Africa, to Calcutta, India.

Christopher Columbus, sailing for Spain, is credited with the discovery of America although he never set foot on its soil. Magellan is credited with the first circumnavigation of the earth. Other Spanish explorers made their marks in parts of what are now the United States, Mexico, and South America.

For France, claims to various parts of North America were the result of the efforts of such men as **Verrazano, Champlain, Cartier, LaSalle, Father Marquette and Joliet**. Dutch claims were based on the work of one **Henry Hudson**. **John Cabot** gave England its stake in North America along with **John Hawkins, Sir Francis Drake, and the half-brothers Sir Walter Raleigh and Sir Humphrey Gilbert**.

Actually the first Europeans in the New World were Norsemen led by **Eric the Red** and later, his son **Leif the Lucky**. But before any of these, the ancestors of today's **Native Americans and Latin American Indians** crossed the Bering Strait from Asia to Alaska, eventually settling in all parts of the Americas.

5.6 Understand the significance of revolutionary movements

The time period of the 1700s and 1800s was characterized in Western countries by the opposing political ideas of **democracy and nationalism**, resulting in strong nationalistic feelings and people of common cultures asserting their belief in the right to have a part in their government.

The **American Revolution** resulted in the successful efforts of the English colonies in America, experienced in over one hundred years of mostly self-government and resentful of increased British meddling and ever-increasing control, in declaring their freedom, winning a war with aid from France, and forming a new independent nation.

The **French Revolution** was the revolt of the middle and lower classes against the gross political and economic excesses of the rulers and the supporting nobility. It ended with the establishment of the First in a series of French Republics. Conditions leading to revolt included extreme taxation; inflation; lack of food; and the total ignoring and disregard for the impossible, degrading, unacceptible condition of the people on the part of the rulers, nobility, and the Church.

The **Industrial Revolution**, which began in Great Britain and spread elsewhere, was the development of power-driven machinery (fueled by coal and steam) leading to the accelerated growth of industry with large factories replacing homes and small workshops as work centers. The lives of people changed drastically and a largely agricultural society changed to an industrial one. In Western Europe, the period of empire and colonialism began as the industrial nations seized and claimed parts of Africa and Asia in an effort to control and provide the raw materials needed to feed the industries and machines in the "mother country". Later developments included power based on electricity and internal combustion, replacing coal and steam.

The **Russian Revolution** occurred first in March (or February on the old calendar) 1917 with the abdication of Tsar Nicholas II and the establishment of a democratic government. But the strength of the Bolsheviks, those who were the extreme Marxists and had a majority in Russia's socialist party, overcame opposition and in November (October on the old calendar) did away with the provisional democratic government and set up the world's first Marxist state. The conditions in Russia in previous centuries led up to this. Russia's harsh climate, tremendous size, and physical isolation from the rest of Europe, along with the brutal despotic rule and control of the tsars over enslaved peasants, contributed to the final conditions leading to revolution. Despite the tremendous efforts of Peter the Great to bring his country up to the social, cultural, and economic standards of the rest of Europe, Russia always remained a hundred years or more behind. Autocratic rule, the existence of the system of serfdom or slavery of the peasants, lack of money, defeats in wars, lack of enough food and food production, little, if any, industrialization--all of these contirbuted to conditions ripe for revolt.

By 1914 Russia's industrial growth was even faster than Germany's and agricultural production was improving, along with better transportation. But the conditions of poverty were horrendous; the Orthodox Church was steeped in and mixed in the political activities; and the absolute rule of the tsar was the order of the day. By the time the nation entered World War I, conditions were just right for revolution. Marxist socialism seemed to be the solution or answer to all the problems. Russia had to stop participation in the war, even though winning a big battle.   Industry could not meet the military's needs, transportation by rail was severely disrupted, and it was most difficult to procure supplies from the Allies. The people had had enough of war, injustice, starvation, poverty, slavery, and cruelty. The support for and strength of the Bolsheviks were mainly in the cities. After two or three years of civil war, fighting foreign invasions, and opposing other revolutionary groups, the Bolsheviks were finally successful in making possible a type of "pre-Utopia" for the workers and the people.

As succeeding **Marxist or Communist** leaders came to power, the effects of this violent revolution were felt all around the earth and until 1989-1991, when Communism eventually gave way to various forms of democracies and free enterprise societies in Eastern Europe and the former Soviet Union, the foreign policies of all free Western nations were directly, immensely affected by the Marxist-Communist ideology. It effect on Eastern Europe and the former Soviet Union was felt politically, economically, socially, culturally, geographically. The people of ancient Russia simply exchanged one autocratic dictatorial system for another and its impact on all of the people on the earth is still being felt to this day.

5.7 Understand the importance of the growth of nationalism

The time period from 1830 to 1914 is characterized by the extraordinary growth and spread of **patriotic pride** in a nation along with intense, wide-spread imperialism. Loyalty to one's nation included national pride; extension and maintenance of sovereign political boundaries; unification of smaller states with common language, history, and culture into a more powerful nation; or smaller national groups who, as part of a larger multi-cultural empire, wished to separate into smaller, political, cultural nations. Examples of major events of this time period resulting from the insurgence of nationalism include:

In the United States, **territorial expansion** occurred in the expansion westward under the banner of **"Manifest Destiny."** Also the U.S. was involved in the War with Mexico, the Spanish-American War, and support of the Latin American colonies of Spain in their revolt for independence. In Latin America, the Spanish colonies were successful in their fight for independence and self-government.

In Europe, Italy and Germany were each totally united into one nation from many smaller states. There were revolutions in Austria and Hungary, the Franco-Prussian War, the dividing of Africa among the strong European nations, interference and intervention of Western nations in Asia, and the breakup of Turkish dominence in the Balkans.

In Africa, France, Great Britain, Italy, Portugal, Spain, Germany, and Belgium controlled all of the continent except Liberia and Ethiopia. In Asia and the Pacific Islands, only

China, Japan, and present-day Thailand (Siam) kept their independence. The others were controlled by the strong European nations.

An additional reason for **European imperialism** was the harsh, urgent demand for the raw materials needed to fuel and feed the great Industrial Revolution. These resources were not available in the huge quantity so desperately needed which necessitated (and rationalized) the partitioning of the continent of Africa and parts of Asia. In turn, these colonial areas would purchase the finished manufactured goods.

5.8 Understand the causes and results of the wars of the 20th century

World War I ▪ 1914 to 1918

Causes were
(a) the surge of nationalism
(b) the increasing strength of military capabilities;
(c) massive colonization for raw materials needed for industrialization and manufacturing
(d) military and diplomatic alliances.

The initial spark which started the conflagration was the assassination of Austrian Archduke Francis Ferdinand and his wife in Sarajevo.

There were a total of 28 nations involved in the war, not including colonies and territories. It began July 28, 1914 and ended November 11, 1918 with the signing of theTreaty of Versailles. Economically, the war cost a total of $337 billion; increased inflation and huge war debts; and caused a loss of markets, goods, jobs, and factories. Politically, old empires collapsed; many monarchies disappeared; smaller countries gained temporary independence; Communists seized power in Russia; and, in some cases, nationalism increased. Socially, total populations decreased because of war deaths and low birth rates; there were millions of displaced persons; villages and farms were destroyed; cities grew; women made significant gains in the work force and the ballot box; there was less social distinction and classes; attitudes completely changed and old beliefs and values were questioned. The peace settlement established the League of Nations to ensure peace, but it failed to do so.

World War II ▪ 1939 to 1945

Causes were
(a) ironically, **the Treaty of Paris**, the peace treaty ending World War I, ultimately led to the second World War. Countries that fought in the first war were either dissatisfied over the "spoils" of war, or were punished so harshly that resentment continued building to an eruption twenty years later.

(b) The **economic problems** of both winners and losers of the first war were never resolved and the world-wide Great Depression of the 1930s dealt the final blow to any immediate rapid recovery. Democratic governments in Europe were severely strained and weakened which in turn gave strength and encouragement to those political movements that were extreme and made promises to end the economic chaos in their countries.

(c) **Nationalism**, which was a major cause of World War I, grew even stronger and seemed to feed the feelings of discontent which became more and more rampant. (d) Because of **unstable economic** conditions and political unrest, harsh dictatorships arose in several of the countries, especially where there was no history of experience in democratic government.

(e) Countries such as Germany, Japan, and Italy began to **aggressively expand their borders** and acquire additional territory.

In all, a total of 59 nations became embroiled in World War II which began September 1, 1939 and ended September 2, 1945. These dates include both the European and Pacific Theaters of war. The horrible tragic results of this second global conflagration were more deaths and more destruction than in any other armed conflict. It completely uprooted and displaced millions of people. The end of the war brought renewed power struggles, especially in Europe and China, with many Eastern European nations as well as China coming under complete control and domination of the Communists, supported and backed by the Soviet Union. With the development of and two-time deployment of an atomic bomb against two Japanese cities, the world found itself in the nuclear age. The peace settlement established the United Nations Organization, still existing and operating today.

Korean War ▪ 1950 to 1953

Causes: Korea was under control of Japan from 1895 to the end of the Second World War in 1945. At war's end, the Soviet and U.S. military troops moved into Korea with the U.S. troops in the southern half and the Soviet troops in the northern half with the 38 degree North Latitude line as the boundary. The General Assembly of the U.N. in 1947 ordered elections throughout all of Korea to select one government for the entire country. The Soviet Union would not allow the North Koreans to vote, so they set up a Communist government there. The South Koreans set up a democratic government but both claimed the entire country. At times there were clashes between the troops from 1948 to 1950. After the U.S. removed its remaining troops in 1949 and announced in early 1950 that Korea was not part of its defense line in Asia, the Communists decided to take action and invaded the south.

Participants were: North and South Korea, United States of America, Australia, New Zealand, China, Canada. France, Great Britain, Turkey, Belgium, Ethiopia, Colombia, Greece, South Africa, Luxembourg, Thailand, the Netherlands, and the Philippines. It was the first war in which a world organization played a major military role and it presented quite a challenge to the U.N. which had only been in existence five years.

The war began June 25, 1950 and ended July 27, 1953. A truce was drawn up and an armistice agreement was signed ending the fighting. A permanent treaty of peace has never been signed and the country remains divided between the Communist North and the Democratic South. It was a very costly and bloody war destroying villages and homes, displacing and killing millions of people.

The Vietnam War
U.S.   Involvement ■ 1957 to 1973

Causes: U.S. involvement was the second phase of three in Vietnam's history. The first phase began in 1946 when the Vietnamese fought French troops for control of the country. Vietnam prior to 1946 had been part of the French colony of Indochina (since 1861 along with Laos and Kampuchea or Cambodia). In 1954 the defeated French left and the country became divided into Communist North and Democratic South. U.S. aid and influence continued as part of U.S. "Cold War" foreign policy to help any nation threatened by Communism.

The second phase involved the U.S. commitment. The Communist Vietnamese considered the war one of national liberation, a struggle to avoid continual dominance and influence of a foreign power. A cease-fire was arranged in January 1973 and a few months later U.S. troops left for good. The third and final phase consisted of fighting between the Vietnamese but ended April 30, 1975, with the surrender of South Vietnam, the entire country being united under Communist rulership.

Participants were the United States of America, Australia, New Zealand, South and North Vietnam, South Korea, Thailand, and the Philippines. With active U.S. involvement from 1957 to 1973, it was the longest war participated in by the U.S.; was tremendously destructive and completely divided the American public in their opinions and feelings about the war. Many were frustrated and angered by the fact that it was the first war fought on foreign soil in which U.S. combat forces were totally unable to achieve their goals and objectives. Returning veterans faced not only readjustment to normal civilian life but also faced bitterness, anger, rejection, and no heroes' welcomes. Many suffered severe physical and deep psychological problems. The war set a precedent with Congress and the American people actively challenging U.S. military and foreign policy. The conflict, though tempered markedly by time, still exists and still has a definite effect on people.

5.9 Show understanding of major contemporary world issues and trends

The struggle between the **Communist world under Soviet Union** leadership and the non-Communist world under Anglo-American leadership resulted in what became known as the Cold War. Communism crept into the Western Hemisphere with Cuban leader Fidel Castro and his regime. Most colonies in Africa, Asia, and the Middle East gained independence from European and Western influence and control. In South Africa in the early 1990s, the system of racial segregation, called "apartheid," was abolished.

The Soviet Union was the first industrialized nation to successfully begin a program of **space flight and exploration**, launching Sputnik and putting the first man in space. The United States also experienced success in its space program successfully landing space crews on the moon. In the late 1980s and early 1990s, the Berlin Wall was torn down and Communism fell in the Soviet Union and Eastern Europe. The 15 republics of the former U.S.S.R. became independent nations with varying degrees of freedom and democracy in government and together formed the Commonwealth of Independent States (CIS). The former Communist nations of Eastern Europe also emphasized their independence with democratic forms of government.

Tremendous progress in communication and transportation has tied all parts of the earth and drawn them closer. There are still vast areas of unproductive land, extreme poverty, food shortages, rampant diseases, violent friction between cultures, the ever-present nuclear threat, environmental pollution, rapid reduction of natural resources, urban over-crowding, acceleration in global terrorism and violent crimes, and a diminishing middle class.

5.10 Know the differences between the world's major religions

Eight major religions practiced today are:

(1) Judaism ▪ the oldest of the eight and was the first to teach and practice the belief in one God, Yahweh.

(2) Christianity ▪ came from Judaism, grew and spread in the First Century throughout the Roman Empire, despite persecution. A later schism resulted in the Western (Roman Catholic) and Eastern (Orthodox) parts. Protestant sects developed as part of the Protestant Revolution. The name "Christian" means one who is a follower of Jesus Christ who started Christianity. Christians follow his teachings and examples, living by the laws and principles of the Bible.

(3) Islam ▪ founded in Arabia by Mohammed who preached on God, Allah. Islam spread through trade, travel, and conquest and followers of it fought in the Crusades

and other wars against Christians and today against the Jewish nation of Israel. Practicers of Islam, called Muslims, live by the teachings of the Koran, their holy book, and of their prophets.

(4) Hinduism ▪ begun by people called Aryans around 1500 B.C. and spread into India. The Aryans blended their culture with the culture of the Dravidians, natives they conquered. Today it has many sects, promotes worship of hundreds of gods and goddesses and belief in reincarnation. Though forbidden today by law, a prominent feature of Hinduism in the past was a rigid adherence to and practice of the infamous caste system.

(5) Buddhism ▪ developed in India from the teachings of Prince Gautama and spread to most of Asia. Its beliefs opposed the worship of numerous deities, the Hindu caste system and the supernatural.. Worshippers must be free of attachment to all things worldly and devote themselves to finding release from life's suffering.

(6) Confucianism is a Chinese religion based on the teachings of the Chinese philosopher Confucius. There is no clergy, no organization, no belief in a deity nor in life after death. It emphasizes political and moral ideas with respect for authority and ancestors. Rulers were expected to govern according to high moral standards.

(7) Taoism ▪ a native Chinese religion with worship of more deities than almost any other religion. It teaches all followers to make the effort to achieve the two goals of happiness and immortality. Practices and ceremonies include meditation, prayer, magic, reciting scriptures, special diets, breath control, beliefs in witchcraft, fortune-telling, astrology, and communicating with the spirits of the dead.

(8) Shinto ▪ the native religion of Japan developed from native folk beliefs worshipping spirits and demons in animals, trees, and mountains. According to its mythology, deities created Japan and its people which resulted in worshipping the emperor as a god. Shinto was strongly influenced by Buddhism and Confucianism but never had strong doctrines on salvation or life after death.

Interestingly, all of these eight major religions have divisions or smaller sects within them. Not one of them is totally completely unified.

6.0 AMERICAN HISTORY

6.1 Understand the importance of the Age of Exploration

The Age of Exploration actually had its beginnings centuries before exploration actually took place. The rise and spread of Islam in the seventh century and its subsequent control over the holy city of Jerusalem led to the European so-called holy wars, the Crusades, to free Jerusalem and the Holy Land from this control. Even though, as a whole, the Crusades were not a success, those who survived and returned to their homes and countries in Western Europe brought back with them new products such as silks, spices, perfumes, new and different foods - luxuries unheard of that gave new meaning to colorless, drab, dull lives.

New ideas, new inventions, and new methods also went to Western Europe with the returning Crusaders and from these new influences was the intellectual stimulation which led to the period known as the Renaissance. Revival of interest in classical Greece led to increased interest in art, architecture, literature, science, astronomy, medicine and increased trade between Europe and Asia plus the invention of the printing press to give the spread of knowledge a big push was all that was needed to start exploring.

For many centuries, various map-makers made many maps and charts which in turn stimulated curiosity and the seeking of more knowledge. At the same time, the Chinese were using the magnetic compass in their sailings. Pacific islanders were going from island to island, covering thousands of miles in open canoes navigating by sun and stars. Arab traders were sailing all over the Indian Ocean in their dhows. The trade routes between Europe and Asia were slow, difficult, dangerous, and very expensive. Between sea voyages on the Indian Ocean and Mediterranean Sea and the camel caravans in central Asis and the Arabian Desert, the trade was still controlled by the Italian merchants in Genoa and Venice. It would take months and even years for the exotic luxuries of Asia to reach the markets of Western Europe. There had to be found a faster cheaper way. And a way had to be found which would by-pass and end the control of the Italian merchants.

Prince Henry of Portugal (also called the Navigator) encouraged, supported, and financed the Portuguese seamen who led in the search for an all-water route to Asia. A shipyard was built along with a school teaching navigation. New types of sailing ships were built which would carry the seamen safely through the ocean waters. Experiments were conducted in newer maps, newer navigational methods, and newer instruments. These included the astrolabe and the compass enabling sailors to determine direction as well as latitude and longitude for exact location. Even though Prince Henry died in 1460, the Portuguese kept on, sailing along and exploring Africa's west coastline. In 1488, Bartholomew Diaz and his men sailed around Africa's southern tip and were headed toward Asia. Diaz wanted to push on but turned back because his men were discouraged and weary from the long months at sea, extremely fearful of the unknown, and just refusing to travel any further. But the Portuguese were finally successful ten years later in 1498 when Vasco da Gama and his men, continuing the route of Diaz, rounded Africa's Cape of Good Hope, sailing across the Indian Ocean, reaching India's port of Calicut (Calcutta). Even though, six years earlier, Columbus had reached the New World and an entire hemisphere, da Gama had proved Asia could be reached from Europe by sea.

Of course, everyone knows that Columbus' first trans-Atlantic voyage was to try to prove his theory or idea that Asia could be reached by sailing west. And to a certain extent his idea was true. It could be done but only after figuring how to go around or across or through the land mass in between. Long after Spain dispatched explorers and her famed conquistadores to gather the wealth for the Spanish monarchs and their coffers, the British were searching valiantly for the "Northwest Passage," a land-sea route across North America and the eventual open sea to the wealth of Asia. It wasn't until after the Lewis and Clark Expedition when Captains Meriwether Lewis and William Clark proved conclusively that there simply was no Northwest Passage. It did not exist.

But this did not deter exploration and settlement. **Spain, France, and England** along with some participation by the **Dutch**, led the way with expanding Western European civilization in the **New World.** These three nations had strong monarchial governments and were struggling for dominance and power in Europe. With the defeat of Spain's mighty Armada in 1588, England became undisputed mistress of the seas. Spain lost its power and influence in Europe and it was left to France and England to carry on the rivalry, leading to eventual British control in Asia as well.

Spain's influence was in Florida, the Gulf Coast from Texas all the west to California and south to the tip of South America and some of the islands of the West Indies. French control centered from New Orleans north to what is now northern Canada including the entire Mississippi Valley, the St. Lawrence Valley, the Great Lakes, and the land that was part of the Louisiana Territory. There were some West Indies islands as part of France's empire also. England settled the eastern seaboard of North America, including parts of Canada and from Maine to Georgia. Some West Indies islands also came under British control. The Dutch had New Amsterdam for a period of time but later ceded it into British hands. Of course, one interesting aspect of all of this was that in each of these three nations, expecially in England, the land claims extended partly or all the way across the continent, regardless of the fact that the others claimed the same land. The wars for dominance and control of power and influence in Europe would undoubtedly and eventually extend to the Americas, especially North America. Which is exactly what happened.

The importance of the Age of Exploration was not only the discovery and colonization of the New World, but also better maps and charts; new accurate navigational instruments; increased knowledge; great wealth; new and different foods and items not known in Europe; a new hemisphere as a refuge from poverty, persecution, a place to start a new and better life; and proof that Asia could be reached by sea and that the earth was round; ships and sailors would not sail off the edge of a flat earth and disappear forever into nothingness.

6.2 Know the significance of the Colonial Period

The part of North America claimed by France was called New France and consisted of the land west of the Appalachian Mountains. This area of claims and settlement included the St. Lawrence Valley, the Great Lakes, the Mississippi Valley, and the entire region of land westward to the Rockies. They established the permanent settlements of Montreal and New Orleans, thus giving them control of the two major gateways into the heart of North America, the vast, rich interior. The St. Lawrence River, the Great Lakes, and the Mississippi River along with its tributaries made it possible for the French explorers and traders to roam at will, virtually unhindered in exploring, trapping, trading, and furthering the interests of France.

Most of the French settlements were in Canada along the St. Lawrence. Only scattered forts and trading posts were found in the upper Mississippi Valley and Great Lakes region. The rulers of France originally intended New France to have vast estates owned by nobles and worked by peasants with the peasants living on the estates in compact farming villages--the New World version of the Old World's medieval system of feudalism. But it didn't work out that way. Each of the nobles wanted his estate to be on the river for ease of transportation. The peasants working the estates wanted the prime waterfront location, also. The result of all this real estate squabbling was that New France's settled areas wound up mostly as a string of farmhouses stretching from Quebec to Montreal along the St. Lawrence and Richelieu Rivers.

In the non-settled areas in the interior were the **French fur traders**. They made friends with the friendly tribes of Indians, spending the winters with them getting the furs needed for trade. In the spring, they would return to Montreal in time to take advantage of trading their furs for the products brought by the cargo ships from France which usually arrived at about the same time. Most of the wealth for New France and its "Mother Country" was from the fur trade, which provided a livelihood for many, many people. Manufacturers and workmen back in France, shipowners and merchants, as well as the fur traders and their Indian allies all benefitted. But the freedom of roaming and trapping in the interior was a strong enticement for the younger, stronger men and resulted in the French not strengthening the areas settled along the St. Lawrence.

Into the 18th century the rivalry with the British was getting stronger and stronger. New France was united under a single government and enjoyed the support of many Indian allies. The French traders were very diligent in not destroying the forests and driving away game upon which the Indians depended for life. It was difficult for the French to defend all of their settlements as they were scattered over half of the continent. But by the early 1750s, in Western Europe, France was the most powerful nation. Its armies were superior to all others and its navy was giving the British stiff competition for control of the seas. The stage was set for confrontation both in Europe and America.

Spanish settlement had its beginnings in the Caribbean with the establishment of colonies on Hispaniola (at Santo Domingo which became the capital of the West Indies), Puerto Rico, and Cuba. There were a number of reasons for Spanish involvement in the Americas, to name just a few:

- the spirit of adventure
- the desire for land
- extension of Spanish power, influence, and empire
- the desire for great wealth
- expansion of Roman Catholic influence and conversion of native peoples

The first permanent settlement in what is now the United States was in 1565 at **St. Augustine**, Florida. A later permanent settlement in the southwestern United States was in 1609 at Santa Fe, New Mexico. At the peak of Spanish power, the area in the United States claimed, settled, and controlled by Spain included Florida and all land west of the Mississippi River--quite a piece of choice real estate. Of course, France and England also lay claim to the same areas. Nonetheless, ranches and missions were built and the Indians who came in contact with the Spaniards were introduced to animals, plants,and seeds from the Old World that they had never seen before. Animals brought in included

- horses
- cattle
- donkeys
- pigs
- sheep
- goats
- poultry

Barrels were cut in half and filled with earth to transport and transplant trees bearing:

apples	olives
oranges	lemons
limes	figs
cherries	apricots
pears	almonds
walnuts	

Even sugar cane and flowers made it to America along with bags bringing seeds of wheat, barley, rye, flax, lentils, rice, and peas.

All Spanish colonies belonged to the king of Spain. He was considered **an absolute monarch** with complete or absolute power and claimed rule by divine right, the belief being God had given him the right to rule and he answered only to God for his actions. His word was final, was the law. The people had no voice in government. The land, the people, the wealth all belonged to him to use as he pleased. He appointed personal representatives, or viceroys, to rule for him in his colonies. They ruled in his name with complete authority. Since the majority of them were friends and advisers, they were richly rewarded with land grants, gold and silver, privileges of trading, and the right to operate the gold and silver mines.

For the needed labor in the mines and on the plantations, Indians were used first as slaves. But they either rapidly died out due to a lack of immunity from European diseases or escaped into nearby jungles or mountains. As a result, African slaves were brought in, expecially to the islands of the West Indies. Some historians state that Latin American slavery was less harsh than in the later English colonies in North America.

Three reasons are given:

(a) the following of a slave code based on ancient Roman laws

(b) the efforts of the Roman Catholic Church to protect and defend slaves because of efforts to convert them

(c) supposedly the existence of less prejudice because of racial mixtures in parts of Spain controlled at one time by dark-skinned Moors from North Africa. Regardless, slavery was still slavery and was very harsh--cruelly denying dignity and human worth and leading to desperate resistance.

Spain's control over her New World colonies lasted more than 300 years, longer than England or France. To this day, Spanish influence remains in names of places, art, architecture, music, literature, law, and cuisine. The Spanish settlements in North America were not commercial enterprises but were for protection and defense of the trading and wealth from their colonies in Mexico and South America. The Russians hunting seals came down the Pacific coast; the English moved into Florida and west into and beyond the Appalachians; and the French traders and trappers were making their way from Louisiana and other parts of New France into Spanish territory. The Spanish never realized or understood that self-sustaining economic development and colonial trade was so important. As a result, the Spanish settlements in the U.S. never really prospered.

The nation had only itself to blame for this. The treasure and wealth found in Spanish New World colonies went back to Spain to be used to buy whatever goods and products were needed instead of setting up industries to make what was needed. As the amount of gold and silver was depleted, Spain could not pay for the goods needed and was unable to produce goods for themselves. Also, at the same time, Spanish treasure ships at sea were being seized by English and Dutch "pirates" taking the wealth to the coffers of their own countries.

It's interesting that before 1763, when England was rapidly on the way to becoming the most powerful of the three major Western European powers, its thirteen colonies, located between the Atlantic and the Appalachians, physically occupied the least amount of land.   And it is also interesting that even before the Spanish Armada was defeated, two Englishmen, Sir Humphrey Gilbert and his half-brother Sir Walter Raleigh, were unsuccessful in their attempts to build successful permanent colonies in the New World. Nonetheless, the thirteen English colonies were successful and, by the time they had gained their independence from Britain, were more than able to govern themselves.   They had a rich historical heritage of law, tradition, and documents leading the way to constitutional government conducted according to laws and customs. The settlers in the British colonies highly valued individual freedom, democratic government, and getting ahead through hard work.

The English colonies, with only a few exceptions, were considered commercial ventures--to make a profit for the crown or the company or whoever financed its beginnings. One was strictly a philanthropic enterprise and three others were primarily for religious reasons but the other nine were started for economic reasons. Settlers in these unique colonies came for different reasons:

- religious freedom
- political freedom
- economic prosperity
- land ownership

The colonies were divided generally into the three regions of New England, Middle Atlantic, and Southern. The culture of each was distinct and affected attitudes, ideas towards politics, religion, and economic activities. The geography of each region also contributed to its unique characteristics.

The New England colonies consisted of Massachusetts, Rhode Island, Connecticut, and New Hampshire. Life in these colonies was centered around the towns. What farming was done was by each family on its own plot of land but a short summer growing season and limited amount of good soil gave rise to other economic activities such as manufacturing, fishing, shipbuilding, and trade. The vast majority of the settlers shared similar origins, coming from England and Scotland. Towns were carefully planned and laid out the same way. The form of government was the town meeting where all adult males met to make the laws. The legislative body, the General Court, consisted of an upper and lower house.

The Middle or Middle Atlantic colonies included New York, New Jersey, Pennsylvania, Delaware, and Maryland. New York and New Jersey were at one time the Dutch colony of New Netherland and Delaware at one time was New Sweden. These five colonies, from their beginnings were considered "melting pots" with settlers from many different nations and backgrounds. The main economic activity was farming with the settlers scattered over the countryside cultivating rather large farms. The Indians were not as much of a threat as in New England so they did not have to settle in small farming villages. The soil was very fertile, the land was gently rolling, and a milder climate provided a longer growing season. These farms produced a large surplus of food, not only for the colonists themselves but also for sale. This colonial region became known as the **"breadbasket"** of the New World and the New York and Philadelphia seaports were constantly filled with ships being loaded with meat, flour, and other foodstuffs for the West Indies and England. There were other economic activities such as shipbuilding, iron mines, and factories producing paper, glass, and textiles. The legislative body in Pennsylvania was unicameral or consisted of one house. In the other four, the legislative body had two houses. Also units of local government were in counties and towns.

The **Southern colonies** were Virginia, North and South Carolina, and Georgia. Virginia was the first permanent successful English colony and Georgia was the last. The year 1619 was a very important year in the history of Virginia and the United States with three very significant events. First, sixty women were sent to Virginia to marry and establish families; second, twenty Africans, the first of thousands, arrived; third, most importantly, the Virginia colonists were granted the right to self-government and they began by electing their own representatives to the House of Burgesses, their own legislative body.

The major economic activity in this region was farming. Here too the soil was very fertile and the climate was very mild with an even longer growing season. The large plantations eventually requiring large numbers of slaves were found in the coastal or tidewater areas. Even though the wealthy slave-owning planters set the pattern of life in this region, most of the people lived inland away from coastal areas. They were small farmers and very few, ir any, owned slaves.

The settlers in these four colonies came from diverse backgrounds and cultures. Virginia was colonized mostly by people from England while Georgia was started as a haven for debtors from English prisons. Pioneers from Virginia settled in North Carolina while South Carolina welcomed people from England and Scotland, French Protestants, Germans, and emigrants from islands in the West Indies. Products from farms and plantations included rice, tobacco, indigo, cotton, some corn and wheat. Other economic activities included lumber and naval stores (tar, pitch, rosin, and turpentine) from the pine forests and fur trade on the frontier. Cities such as Savannah and Charleston were important seaports and trading centers.

In the colonies, the daily life of the colonists differed greatly between the coastal settlements and the inland or interior. The Southern planters and the people living in the coastal cities and towns had a way of life similar to that in towns in England. The influence was seen and heard in how people dressed and talked, the architectural styles of houses and public buildings, and the social divisions or levels of society. Both the planters and city dwellers enjoyed an active social life and had strong emotional ties to England.

On the other hand, life inland on the frontier had marked differences. All facets of daily living--clothing, food, home, economic and social activities--were all connected to what was needed to sustain life and survive in the wilderness. Everything was produced practically themselves. They were self-sufficient and extremely individualistic and independent. There was little, if any, levels of society or class distinctions as they considered themselves to be the equal to all others, regardless of station in life. The roots of equality, independence, individual rights and freedoms were extremely strong and well-developed. People were not judged by their fancy dress, expensive house, eloquent language, or titles following their names.

The colonies had from 1607 to 1763 to develop, refine, practice, experiment, and experience life in a rugged, uncivilized land. The Mother Country had virtually left them on their own to take care of themselves all that time. So when in 1763 Britain decided she needed to regulate and "mother" the "little ones," to her surprise, she had a losing fight on her hands.

6.3 Explain the crucial effects of the period of the American Revolution

By the 1750s in Europe, Spain was "out of the picture," no longer the most powerful nation and not even a contender. The remaining rivalry was between Britain and France. For nearly 25 years, between 1689 and 1748, a series of "armed conflicts" involving these two powers had been taking place. These conflicts had spilled over into North America. The War of the League of Augsburg in Europe, 1689 to 1697, had been King William's War. The War of the Spanish Succession, 1702 to 1713, had been Queen Anne's War. The War of the Austrian Succession, 1740 to 1748, was called King George's War in the colonies. The two nations fought for possession of colonies, especially in Asia and North America, and for control of the seas, but none of these conflicts were decisive.

The final conflict, which decided once and for all who was the most powerful, began in North America in 1754, in the Ohio River Valley. It was known in America as the French and Indian War and in Europe as the Seven Years War, since it began there in 1756. In America, both sides had advantages and disadvantages. The British colonies were well-established and consolidated in a smaller area. British colonists outnumbered French colonists 23 to 1. Except for a small area in Canada, French settlements were scattered over a much larger area (roughly half of the continent) and were smaller. However, the French settlements were united under one government and were quick to act and cooperate together when necessary. Also the French had many more Indian allies than the British. The British colonies had separate, individual governments and very seldom cooperated together, even when needed. Too, in Europe, at that time, France was the more powerful of the two nations.

Both sides had stunning victories and humiliating defeats. If there was one person who could be given the credit for British victory, it would have to be William Pitt. He was a strong leader, enormously energetic, supremely self-confident, and absolutely determined on a complete British victory. Despite the advantages and military victories of the French, Pitt succeeded. In the army he got rid of the incompetents and replaced them with men who could do the job. He sent more troops to America, strengthened the British navy, gave to the officers of the colonial militias equal rank to the British officers - in short, he saw to it that Britain took the offensive and kept it to victory. Of all the British victories, perhaps the most crucial and important was winning Canada.

The French depended on the St. Lawrence River for transporting supplies, soldiers, and messages—the link between New France and the Mother Country. Tied into this waterway system were the connecting links of the Great Lakes, Mississippi River and its tributaries along which were scattered French forts, trading posts, and small settlements. When, in 1758, the British captured Louisburg on Cape Breton Island, New France was doomed. Louisburg gave the British navy a base of operations preventing French reinforcements and supplies getting to their troops. Other forts fell to the British: Frontenac, Duquesne, Crown Point, Ticonderoga, Niagara, those in the upper Ohio Valley, and, most importantly, Quebec and finally Montreal. Spain entered the war in 1762 to aid France but it was too late. British victories occurred all around the world: in India, in the Mediterranean, and in Europe.

In 1763 in Paris, Spain, France, and Britain met to draw up the Treaty. Great Britain got most of India and all of North America east of the Mississippi River, except for New Orleans. Britain received from Spain control of Florida and returned to Spain Cuba and the islands of the Philippines, taken during the war. France lost nearly all of its possessions in America and India and were allowed to keep four islands: Guadeloupe, Martinique, Haiti on Hispaniola, and Miquelon and St. Pierre. France gave Spain New Orleans and the vast territory of Louisiana, west of the Mississippi River. Britain was now the most powerful nation--period.

Where did all of this leave the British colonies? Their colonial militias had fought with the British and they too benefitted. The militias and their officers gained much experience in fighting which was very valuable later on. The thirteen colonies began to realize that cooperating with each other was the only way to defend themselves. They didn't really understand that, until the war for independence and setting up a national government, but a start had been made. At the start of the war in 1754, Benjamin Franklin proposed to the thirteen colonies that they unite together permanently to be able to defend themselves. This was after the French and their Indian allies had defeated Major George Washington and his militia at Fort Necessity. This left all of the northern frontier of the British colonies vulnerable and open to attack.

Delegates from seven of the thirteen colonies met at Albany, New York, along with the representatives from the Iroquois Confederation and British officials. Franklin's proposal, known as the Albany Plan of Union, was totally rejected by the colonists, along with a similar proposal from the British. They simply did not want each of the colonies to lose its right to act independently. But the seed was planted.

The war for independence occurred due to a number of changes, the two most important ones being economic and political. By the end of the French and Indian War in 1763, Britain's American colonies were thirteen out of a total of thirty-three scattered around the earth. Like all other countries, Britain strove for having a strong economy and a favorable balance of trade. To have that delicate balance a nation needs wealth, self-sufficiency, and a powerful army and navy. This is where the overseas colonies came into the picture. They would provide raw materials for the industries in the Mother Country, be a market for the finished products by buying them and assist the Mother Country in becoming powerful and strong (as in the case of Great Britain) by having a strong merchant fleet which would be a school for training for the Royal Navy and provide places as bases of operation for the operation of the Royal Navy.

The foregoing explained the major reason for British encouragement and support of colonization, especially in North America. So between 1607 and 1763, at various times for various reasons, the British Parliament enacted different lawd to assist the government in getting and keeping this trade balance. One series of laws required that most of the manufacturing be done only in England, such as: prohibition of exporting any wool or woolen cloth from the colonies; no manufacture of beaver hats or iron products. The colonists weren't concerned as they had no money and no highly skilled labor to set up any industries, anyway.

The Navigation Acts of 1651 put restrictions on shipping and trade within the British Empire by requiring that it was allowed only on British ships. This increased the strength of the British merchant fleet and greatly benefitted the American colonists. Since they were British citizens they could have their own vessels, building and operating them as well. By the end of the war in 1763, the shipyards in the colonies were building one third of the merchant ships under the British flag. There were quite a number of wealthy American colonial merchants.

The Navigation Act of 1660 restricted the shipment and sale of colonial products to England only. In 1663 another Navigation Act stipulated that the colonies had to buy manufactured products only from England and that any European goods going to the colonies had to go to England first. These were a protection--from enemy ships and pirates and from competition from European rivals.

The New England and Middle Atlantic colonies at first felt threatened by these laws as they had started producing many of the products already being produced in Britain. But they soon found new markets for their goods and began what was known as a "triangular trade." Colonial vessels started the first part of the triangle by sailing for Africa loaded with kegs of rum from colonial distilleries. On Africa's west coast the rum was traded for either gold or slaves. The second or next part of the triangle was from Africa to the West Indies where the slaves were traded for molasses, sugar, or money. The third and last part of the triangle was home, bringing sugar or molasses (to make more rum) and gold and silver.

The major concern of the British government was that the trade violated the 1733 Molasses Act. Planters had wanted the colonists to buy all of their molasses in the British West Indies but these islands could give the traders only about one eighth of the amount of molasses needed for distilling the rum. The colonists were forced to buy the rest of what they needed from the French, Dutch, and Spanish islands, thus evading the law by not paying the high duty on the molasses bought from these islands. If Britain had enforced the Molasses Act, economic and financial chaos and ruin would have occurred. But for this act and all the other mercantile laws, the government followed the policy of "salutary neglect," deliberately failing to enforce the laws.

In 1763, after the war, money was needed to pay the British war debt, for the defense of the empire, and to pay for the governing of 33 colonies scattered around the earth. It was decided to adopt a new colonial policy and pass laws to raise revenue. After all, it was reasoned, the colonists were subjects of the king and since the king and his ministers had spent a great deal of money defending and protecting them (this especially for the American colonists), it was only right and fair that the colonists should

help pay the costs of defense, especially theirs. The earlier laws passed had been for the purposes of regulating production and trade which generally put money into colonial pockets. These new laws would take some of that rather hard-earned money out of their pockets and it would be done, in colonial eyes, unjustly and illegally.

Before 1763, except for trade and supplying raw materials, the colonies had been left pretty much to themselves. England looked on them merely as part of an economic or commercial empire. Little consideration was given as to how they were to conduct their daily affairs, so the colonists became very independent, self-reliant, and extremely skillful at handling those daily affairs. This, in turn, gave rise to leadership, initiative, achievement, and vast experience. In fact, there was a far greater degree of independence and self-government in the British colonies in America than could be found in Britain or the major countries on the Continent or any other colonies anywhere. There were a number of reasons for this:

One, the religious and scriptural teachings of previous centuries put forth the worth of the individual and equality in God's sight. Keep in mind that freedom of worship and from religious persecution were major reasons to live in the New World.

Two, European Protestants, especially Calvinists, believed and taught the idea that government originates from those governed, that rulers are required to protect individual rights and that the governed have the right and privilege to choose their rulers.

Three, trading companies put into practice the principle that their members had the right to make the decisions and shape the policies affecting their lives.

Four, the colonists believed and supported th idea that a person's property should not be taken without his consent, based on that treasured English document, Magna Carta, and English common law.

Five, from about 1700 to 1750, population increases in America came about throught immigration and generations and generations of descendants of the original settlers. The immigrants were mainly Scots-Irish who hated the English, Germans who cared nothing about England, and black slaves who knew nothing about England. The descendants of the original settlers had never been out of America at any time.

Six, in America, as new towns and counties were formed, there began the practice of representation in government. Representatives to the colonial legislative assemblies were elected from the district in which they lived, chosen by qualified property-owning male voters, and representing the interests of the political district from which they were elected. One thing to remember: each of the 13 colonies had a royal governor appointed by the king, representing his interests in the colonies. But the colonial legislative assemblies controlled the purse strings having the power to vote on all issues involving money to be spent by the colonial governments.

Contrary and opposite to this was the governmental set-up in England. Members of Parliament were not elected to represent their own districts. They were considered representative of classes, not individuals. If some members of a professional or commercial class or some landed interests were able to elect representatives, then those classes or special interests were represented. It had nothing at all to do with numbers or territories. Some large population centers had no direct representation at all, yet the people there considered themselves represented by men elected from their particular class or interest somewhere else. Consequently, it was extremely difficult for the English to understand why the American merchants and landowners claimed they were not represented because they themselves did not vote for a member of Parliament.

The colonists' protest of "no taxation without representation" was meaningless to the English. Parliament represented the entire nation, was completely unlimited in legislation, and had become supreme; and the colonists were incensed at the English attitude of "of course you have representation--everyone does." The colonists considered their colonial legislative assemblies equal to Parliament, totally unacceptable in England, of course. There were two different environments of the older traditional British system in the Mother Country and in America, new ideas and different ways of doing things. In a new country, a new environment has little or no tradition, institutions or vested interests. New ideas and traditions grown extremely fast pushing aside what is left of the old ideas and old traditions. So by 1763, Britain had changed its perception of its American colonies to their being a "territorial" empire. The stage was set and the conditions were right for a showdown.

It all began in 1763 when Parliament decided to have a standing army in North America to reinforce British control. In 1765 the Quartering Act was passed requiring the colonists to provide supplies and living quarters for the British troops. In addition, efforts by the British were made to keep the peace by establishing good relations with the Indians. As a result, a proclamation was issued which prohibited any American colonists from making any settlements west of the Appalachians until provided for through treaties with the Indians. The Sugar Act of 1764 required efficient collection of taxes on any molasses that were brought into the colonies and gave British officials free license to conduct searches of the premises of anyone suspected of violating the law. The colonists were taxed on newspapers, legal documents, and other printed matter under the Stamp Act of 1765. Even though a stamp tax was already in use in England, the colonists would have none of it and after the ensuing uproar of rioting and mob violence, Parliament repealed the tax.

Of course, great exultation, jubilence, wild joy resulted when news of the repeal reached America.   But what no one noticed was the small, quiet Declaratory Act attached to the repeal. This act plainly, unequivocally stated that Parliament still had the right to make all laws for the colonies and denied their right to be taxed only by their own colonial legislatures--a very crucial, important piece of legislation but virtually overlooked and unnoticed at the time. Other acts leading up to armed conflict included the Townshend Acts passed in 1767 taxing lead, paint, paper, and tea brought into the colonies.   This really increased anger and tension resulting in the British sending troops to New York City and Boston. In Boston, mob violence provoked retaliation by the troops thus bringing about the deaths of five people and the wounding of eight others. The so-called Boston Massacre shocked Americans and British alike so in 1770, Parliament voted to repeal all of the provisions of the Townshend Acts except the tax on tea.   In 1773, the tax on tea sold by the British East India Company was substantially reduced, fueling colonial anger once more. This gave the company an unfair trade advantage and forcibly reminded the colonists of the British right to tax them.   Merchants refused to sell the tea; colonists refused to buy and drink it; and a shipload of it was dumped into Boston harbor--a most violent Tea Party.

In 1774 the passage of the Quebec Act extended the limits of that Canadian colony's boundary southward to include territory located north of the Ohio River.   But the punishment for Boston's Tea Party came in the same year with the Intolerable Acts. Boston's port was closed; the royal governor of the colony of Massachusetts was given increased power, and the colonists were compelled to house and feed the British soldiers. The propaganda activities of the patriot organizations Sons of Liberty and Committees of Correspondence kept the opposition and resistance before everyone. Delegates from twelve colonies met in Philadelphia September 5, 1774, in the First Continental Congress. They definitely opposed acts of lawlessness and wanted some form of peaceful settlement with Britain.   They maintained American loyalty to the Mother Country and affirmed Parliament's power over colonial foreign affairs. But they insisted on repeal of the Intolerable Acts and demanded ending all trade with Britain until this took place. The reply from George III, last king of America, was an insistence of colonial submission to British rule or be crushed. With the start of the Revolutionary War April 19, 1775, the Second Continental Congress began meeting in Philadelphia May 10th of that year to conduct the business of war and government for the next six years.

Interestingly, one historian explained that the British were interested only in raising money to pay war debts, regulate the trade and commerce of the colonies, and look after business and financial interests between the Mother Country and the rest of her empire. The establishment of overseas colonies was first and foremost a commercial enterprise, not a political one. The political aspect was secondary and assumed. The British took it for granted that Parliament was supreme, was recognized so by the colonists, and were very resentful of the colonial challenge to Parliament's authority. They were contemptuously indifferent to politics in America and had no wish to exert any control over it but as resistance and disobedience swelled and increased in America, the British increased their efforts to punish them and put them in their place.

The British had been extremely lax and totally inconsistant in enforcement of the mercantile or trade laws passed in the years before 1754. The government itself was not particularly stable so actions against the colonies occurred in anger and their attitude was one of a moral superiority, that they knew how to manage America better than the Americans did themselves. This of course points to a lack of sufficient knowledge of conditions and opinions in America. The colonists had been left on their own for nearly 150 years and by the time the Revolutionary War began, they were quite adept at self-government and adequately handling the affairs of their daily lives, with no one looking over the shoulder telling how and what to do. The Americans equated ownership of land or property with the right to vote. Property was considered the foundation of life and liberty and, in the colonial mind and tradition, these went together. Therefore when an indirect tax on tea was made, the British felt that since it wasn't a direct tax, there should be no objection to it. The colonists viewed any tax, direct or indirect, as an attack on their property. They felt that as a representative body, the British Parliament should protect British citizens, including the colonists, from arbitrary taxation. But since they felt they were not represented, Parliament, in their eyes, gave them no protection. So, war began.

August 23, 1775, George III declared that the colonies were in rebellion and warned them to stop or else. By 1776 the colonists and their representatives in the Second Continental Congress realized that things were past the point of no return. The Declaration of Independence was drafted and declared July 4, 1776. George Washington labored against tremendous odds to wage a victorious war. The turning point in the Americans' favor occurred in 1777 with the American victory at Saratoga. This decided the French to align themselves with the Americans against the British. With the aid of Admiral deGrasse and French warships blocking the entrance to Chesapeake Bay, British General Cornwallis trapped at Yorktown, Virginia, surrendered in 1781 and the war was over. The Treaty of Paris officially ending the war was signed in 1783.

During the war, after independence was declared, the former colonies now found themselves independent states. The Second Continental Congress was conducting a war with representation by delegates from thriteen separate states. The Congress had no power to act for the states nor to require them to accept and follow its wishes. A permanent united government was desperately needed. On November 15, 1777, the Articles of Confederation were adopted, creating a league of free and independent states. The central government of the new United States of America consisted of a Congress of two to seven delegates from each state with each state having just one vote. The government under the Articles solved some of the postwar problems but had serious weaknesses. Some of its powers included: borrowing and coining money, directing foreign affairs, declaring war and making peace, building and equipping a navy, regulating weights and measures, asking the states to supply men and money for an army. The delegates to Congress had no real authority as each state carefully and jealously guarded its own interests and limited powers under the Articles. Also, the delegates to Congress were paid by their states and had to vote as directed by their state legislatures. The serious weaknesses were the lack of power: to regulate finances, over interstate trade, over foreign trade, to enforce treaties, and military power. Something better and more efficient was needed. In May of 1787, delegates from all states except Rhode Island, began meeting in Philadelphia. At first they met to revise the Articles of Confederation as instructed by Congress; but they soon realized that much more was needed. Abandoning the instructions, they set out to write a new Constitution, a new document, the foundation of all government in the United States and a model for representative government throughout the world.

The first order of business was the agreement among all the delegates that the convention would be kept secret. No discussion of the convention outside of the meeting room would be allowed. They wanted to be able to discuss, argue, and agree among themselves before presenting the completed document to the American people. They were afraid that if the people were aware of what was taking place before it was completed, the entire country would be plunged into argument and dissension and that it would be extremely difficult, if not impossible, to settle differences and come to an agreement. Between the official notes kept and the complete notes of future President James Madison, an accurate picture of the events of the Convention is part of the historical record. The delegates went to Philadelphia representing different areas and different interests. They all agreed on a strong central government but not one with unlimited powers. They also agreed that no one section or part of government could control the rest. It would be a republican form of government (sometimes referred to as representative democracy) in which the supreme power was in the hands of the voters who would elect the men who would govern for them.

One of the first serious controversies involved the small states versus the large states over representation in Congress. Virginia's Governor Edmund Randolph proposed that state population determine the number of representatives sent to Congress, also known as the Virginia Plan. New Jersey delegate William Paterson countered with what is known as the New Jersey Plan, each state having equal representation. After much argument and debate, the Great Compromise was devised, known also as the Connecticut Compromise, as proposed by Roger Sherman. It was agreed that Congress would have two houses. The Senate would have two Senators, giving equal powers in the Senate. The House of Representatives would have its members elected based on each state's population. Both houses could draft bills to debate and vote on with the exception of bills pertaining to money, which must originate in the House of Representatives.

Another major controversy involved economic differences between North and South. One concerned the counting of the African slaves for determining representation in the House of Representatives. The southern delegates wanted this but didn't want it to apply to determining taxes to be paid. The northern delegates argued the opposite: count the slaves for taxes but not for representation. The resulting agreement was known as the "three-fifths" comromise. Three-fifths of the slaves would be counted for both taxes and determining representation in the House.

The last major compromise, also between north and south, was the Commerce Compromise. The economic interests of the northern part of the country were ones of industry and business whereas the south's economic interests were primarily in farming. The northern merchants wanted the government to regulate and control commerce with foreign nations and with the states. Of course, southern planters opposed this idea as they felt that any tariff laws passed would be unfavorable to them. The acceptable compromise to this dispute was that Congress was given the power to regulate commerce with other nations and the states, including levying tariffs on imports. However, Congress did not have the power to levy tariffs on any exports. This increased southern concern about the effect this would have on the slave trade. So the delegates finally agreed that the importation of slaves would continue for 20 more years with no interference from Congress. Any import tax could not exceed 10 dollars per person. After 1808, Congress would be able to decide whether to prohibit or regulate any further importation of slaves.

Of course, when work was completed and the document was presented, nine states needed to approve for it to go into effect. There was no little amount of discussion, arguing, debating, and haranguing. The opposers had three major objections: the states seemed as if they were being asked to surrender too much power to the national government; the voters did not have enough control and influence over the men who would be elected by them to run the government; and a lack of a "bill of rights" guaranteeing hard-won individual freedoms and liberties. Eleven states finally ratified the document and the new national government went into effect. It was no small feat that the delegates were able to produce a workable document that satisfied all opinions, feelings, and viewpoints. The separation of powers of the three branches of government and the built-in system of checks and balances to keep power balanced was a stroke of genius. It provided for the individuals and the states as well as an organized central authority to keep a new inexperienced young nation on track. They created a system of government so flexible that it had continued in its basic form to this day. In 1789 the Electoral College unanimously elected George Washington as the first President and the new nation was on its way.

6.4 Understand how the new nation developed from 1791 to 1860

Beginning with Washington's election to the Presidency in 1791 to the election of Abraham Lincoln in 1860, the United States had expanded to the boundaries of today's 48 conterminous states. During that 69-year period, four wars were fought: the War of 1812 with Great Britain, the war with the Barbary pirates in the Mediterranean, the war with Mexico, and the Seminole wars in Florida. Domestically, by 1860, the nation had had 15 presidents (Lincoln was the 16th), had greatly increased its area, established and strengthened the federal court system, saw the beginnings of and increased influence of political parties, the first and second U.S. banks, economic "panics"or depressions, the abolition movement, the controversies and turmoil leading to the Civil War. There were 33 states in the Union by 1860.

Territorial expansion began in 1783 with the signing of the Treaty of Paris ending the Revolutionary War. According to the terms of the treaty, the land gained by the Americans was all of the land between the Appalachian Mountains and the Mississippi River; from the Great Lakes to the Florida boundary. Nine additional states were formed from this area alone.

The next large territorial gain was under President Thomas Jefferson in 1803. In 1800, Napoleon Bonaparte of France secured the Louisiana Territory from Spain, who had held it since 1792. The vast area stretched westward from the Mississsppi River to the Rocky Mountains as well as northward to Canada. An effort was made to keep the transaction a secret but the news reached the U.S. State Department. The U.S. didn't have any particular problem with Spanish control of the territory since Spain was weak and did not pose a threat. But it was different with France. Though not the world power that Great Britain was, nonetheless France was still strong and, under Napoleon's leadership, was once again aquiring an empire. President Jefferson had three major reasons for concern:

(a) With the French controlling New Orleans at the mouth of the Mississippi River, as well as the Gulf of Mexico, westerners would lose their "right of deposit" which would greatly affect their ability to trade. This was very important to these Americans who were living in the area between the river and the Appalachians. They were unable to get heavy products to eastern markets but had to float them on rafts down the Ohio and

Mississippi Rivers to New Orleans to ships heading to Europe or the Atlantic coast ports. If France prohibited this, it would be a financial disaster.

(b) President Jefferson also worried that if the French possessed the Louisiana Territory, America would be extremely limited in its expansion into its interior.

(c) under Napoleon Bonaparte, France was becoming more powerful and aggressive and this would be a constant worry and threat to the western border of the U.S.President Jefferson was very interested in the western part of the country and firmly believed that it was both necessary and desirable to strengthen western lands. So Jefferson wrote to American minister to Paris Robert R. Livingston to make an offer to Napoleon for New Orleans and West Florida, as much as $10 million for the two. Napoleon countered the offer with the question of how much the U.S. would be willing to pay for all of Louisiana. After some discussion, it was agreed to pay $15 million and the largest land transaction in history was negotiated in 1803, resulting in the eventual formation of 15 states.

In 1804, the United States engaged in the first of a series of armed conflicts with the Barbary pirates of North Africa. The Moslem rulers of Morocco, Algiers, Tunis, and Tripoli--the Barbary States of North Africa--had long been seizing ships of nations that were Christian and demanding ransoms for the crews. The Christian nations of Europe decided it was cheaper and easier to pay annually a tribute or bribe. The U.S. had been doing this also since 1783 with the beginnings of trade between the Mediterranean countries and the newly independent nation. But when the rulers in Tripoli demanded a ridiculously exorbitant bribe and even chopped down the flagpole of the American consulate there, Jefferson had had enough. The first skirmish against Tripoli in 1804 and 1805 was successful and the final end of payment of bribes to all of the rulers came in 1815 after the War of 1812 ended. The Americans could trade and sail freely in the Mediterranean.

United States' unintentional and accidental involvement in what was known as the War of 1812 came about due to the political and economic struggles between France and Great Britain. Napoleon's goal was complete conquest and control of Europe, including and especially Great Britain. Even though British troops were temporarily driven off the mainland of Europe, the navy still controlled the seas, the seas across which France had to bring the products needed. America traded with both nations, especially with France and its colonies. The British decided to destroy the American trade with France, mainly for two reasons: (a) Products and goods from the U.S. gave Napoleon what he needed to keep up his struggle with Britain. He and France were the enemy and it was felt that the Americans were aiding the Mother Country's enemy. (b) Britain felt threatened by the increasing strength and success of the U.S. merchant fleet. They were becoming major competitors with the shipowners and merchants in Britain.

The British issued the Orders in Council which were a series of measures prohibiting American ships from entering any French ports, not only in Europe but also in India and the West Indies.   At the same time Napoleon began efforts for a coastal blockade of the British Isles. He issued a series of Orders prohibiting all nations, including the United States, from trading with the British. And he didn't stop there. He threatened seizure of every ship entering any French ports after they stopped at any British port or British colony, even threatening to seize every ship inspected by British cruisers or that paid any duties to their government. Adding to all of this, the British were stopping American ships and seizing, or impressing, American seamen to service on British ships. Americans were outraged..

In 1807, Congress passed the Embargo Act, forbidding American ships from sailing to foreign ports.   It couldn't be completely enforced and it really hurt business and trade in America so, in 1809, it was repealed. Two additional acts passed by Congress after James Madison became president attempted to regulate trade with other nations and to get Britain and France to remove all the restrictions they had put on American shipping. The catch was that whichever nation removed restrictions, the U.S. agreed not to trade with the other one. Clever Napoleon was the first to do this, prompting Madison to issue orders prohibiting trade with Britain, ignoring warnings from the British not to do so. Of course this didn't work either and even though Britain eventually rescinded the Orders in Council, war came in June of 1812 and ended Christmas Eve, 1814, with the signing of the Treaty of Ghent.

During the war, Americans were divided over not only whether or not it was necessary to even fight but also over what territories should be fought for and taken.   The nation was still young and just not prepared for war. The primary American objective was to conquer Canada but it failed. Two naval and one military victories stand out for the U.S. Oliver Perry gained control of Lake Erie and Thomas Macdonough fought on Lake Champlain, both of these naval battles successfully preventing the British invasion of the United States from Canada. But the troops did land below Washington on the Potomac, marched into the city, and burned the public buildings, including the White House. Andrew Jackson's victory at New Orleans was a great morale booster to Americans, giving them the impression the U.S. had won the war. The battle actually took place after Britain and the United States had reached agreement and it made no difference to the war's outcome. The peace treaty did little for the United States other than bringing peace, releasing prisoners of war, restoring all occupied territory, and setting up a commission to settle boundary disputes with Canada. Interestingly, the war proved to be a turning point in American history. European events had profoundly shaped U.S. policies, especially foreign policies. After 1815, the U.S. became much more independent from European influence and began to be treated with growing respect by European nations who were impressed by the fact that the young United States showed no hesitancy in going to war with the world's greatest naval power.

The Red River cession was the next acquisition of land and came about as part of a treaty with Great Britain in 1818. It included parts of North and South Dakota and Minnesota. In 1819, Florida, both East and West, was ceded to the U.S. by Spain along with parts of Alabama, Mississippi, and Louisiana. Texas was annexed in 1845 and after the war with Mexico in 1848, the government paid $15 million for what became the states of California, Utah, and Nevada and parts of four other states. In 1846 the Oregon Country was ceded to the U.S. which extended the western border to the Pacific Ocean. The northern U.S. boundary was established at the 49th parallel. The states of Idaho, Oregon, and Washington were formed from this territory. In 1853 the Gadsden Purchase rounded out the present boundary of the 48 conterminous states with payment to Mexico of $10 million for land that makes up the present states of New Mexico and Arizona.

In domestic affairs of the new nation, the first problems dealt with finances--paying for the war debts of the Revolutionary War and other financial needs. Secretary of the Treasury Alexander Hamilton wanted the government to increase tariffs and put taxes on certain products made in the U.S., for example, liquor. This money in turn would be used to pay war debts of the federal government as well as those of the states. There would be money available for expenses and needed internal improvements. To provide for this, Hamilton favored a national bank. Secretary of State Thomas Jefferson, along with southern supporters, opposed many of Hamilton's suggested plans. Later, Jefferson relented and gave support to some proposals in return for Hamilton and his northern supporters agreeing to locate the nation's capital in the South. Jefferson continued to oppose a national bank but Congress set up the first one in 1791, chartered for the next 20 years. In 1794 Pennsylvania farmers, who made whiskey, their most important source of cash, refused to pay the liquor tax and started what came to be known as the Whiskey Rebellion. Troops sent by President Washington successfully put it down with no lives lost, thus demonstrating the growing strength of the new government.

The Judiciary Act set up the U.S. Supreme Court by providing for a Chief Justice and five associate justices. It also established federal district and circuit courts. One of the most important acts of Congress was the first 10 amendments to the Constitution called the Bill of Rights which emphasized and gave attention to the rights of individuals.

Under President John Adams, a minor diplomatic upset occurred with the government of France. By this time the two major political parties called Federalists and Democratic-Republicans had fully developed. Hamilton and his mostly Northern followers had formed the Federalist Party, which favored a strong central government and was sympathetic to Great Britain and its interests. The Democratic-Republican Party had been formed by Jefferson and his mostly Southern followers and they wanted a weak central government and stronger relations with and support of France. In 1798 the Federalists, in control of Congress, passed the Alien and Sedition Acts, written to silence vocal opposition. These acts made it a crime to voice any criticism of the President or Congress and unfairly treated all foreigners.

The legislatures of Kentucky and Virginia protested these laws, claiming they attacked freedoms and challenging their constitutionality. These Resolutions stated mainly the states had created the federal government which was considered merely as an agent for the states and was limited to certain powers and could be criticized by the states, if warranted. They went further stating that states' rights included the power to declare any act of Congress null and void if the states felt it unconstitutional. The controversy died down as the Alien and Sedition Acts expired, one by one, but the doctrine of states' rights was not finally settled until the Civil War.

Supreme Court Chief Justice John Marshall made extremely significant contributions to the American judiciary. He set or established three basic principles of law which became the foundation of the judicial system and the federal government.

(a) He started the power of judicial review, the right of the Supreme Court to determine the constitutionality of laws passed by Congress.

(b) He stated that only the Supreme Court had the power to set aside laws passed by state legislatures when they contradicted the U.S. Constitution.

(c) He established the right of the Supreme Court to reverse decisions of state courts.

After the U.S. purchased the Louisiana Territory, Jefferson appointed Captains Meriwether Lewis and William Clark to explore it, to find out exactly what had been bought. The expedition went all the way to the Pacific Ocean, returning two years later with maps, journals, and artifacts. This led the way for future explorers to make available more knowledge about the territory and resulted in the Westward Movement and the later belief in the doctrine of Manifest Destiny.

The election of Andrew Jackson as President signaled a swing of the political pendulum from government influence of the wealthy, aristocratic Easterners to the interests of the Western farmers and pioneers and the era of the "common man." Jacksonian democracy was a policy of equal political power for all. After the War of 1812, Henry Clay and supporters favored economic measures which came to be known as the American System. This involved tariffs protecting American farmers.and manufacturers from having to compete with foreign products, stimulating industrial growth and employment. With more people working, more farm products would be consumed, prosperous farmers would be able to buy more manufactured goods, and the additional monies from tariffs would make it possible for the government to make the needed internal improvements. To get all of this going, in 1816, Congress not only passed a high tariff, but also chartered a second Bank of the United States. So upon becoming President, Jackson fought to get rid of the bank. One of the many duties of the bank was to regulate the supply of money for the nation. The President believed that the bank was a monopoly which favored the wealthy. Congress voted in 1832 to renew the bank's charter but Jackson vetoed the bill, withdrew the government's money, and the bank finally collapsed.

Jackson also faced the "null and void," or nullification issue from South Carolina. Congress, in 1828, passed a law placing high tariffs on goods imported into the United States. Southerners, led by South Carolina's then Vice-President of the U.S. John C. Calhoun, felt that the tariff favored the manufacturing interests of New England, denounced it as an abomination, and claimed that any state could nullify any of the federal laws it considered unconstitutional. The tariff was lowered in 1832, but not low enough to satisfy South Carolina, which promptly threatened to secede from the Union. Although Jackson agreed with the rights of states, he also believed in preservation of the Union. A year later, the tariffs were lowered and the crisis was averted.

Many social reform movements began during this period, including education, women's rights, labor and working conditions, temperance, prisons and insane asylums. But the most intense and controversial was the abolitionists' efforts to end slavery, an effort alienating and splitting the country, hardening Southern defense of slavery, and leading to four years of bloody war. The abolitionist movement had political fallout, affecting admittance of states into the Union and the government's continued efforts to keep a balance between total numbers of free and slave states. Congressional legislation after 1820 reflected this.

The Industrial Revolution had spread from Great Britain to the United States. Before 1800, most manufacturing activities were done in small shops or in homes. But starting in the early 1800s, factories with modern machines were built making it easier to produce goods faster. The eastern part of the country became a major industrial area although some developed in the West. At about the same time, improvements began to be made in building roads, railroads, canals, and steamboats. The increased ease of travel facilitated the westward movement as well as boosted the economy with faster and cheaper shipment of goods and products, covering larger and larger areas. Some of the innovations include the Erie Canal connecting the interior and Great Lakes with the Hudson River and the coastal port of New York. Many other natural waterways were connected by canals.

Robert Fulton's "Clermont," the first commercially successful steamboat, led the way in the fastest way to ship goods, making it the most important way to do so. Later, steam-powered railroads soon became the biggest rival of the steamboat as a means of shipping, eventually being the most important transportation method opening up the West. With expansion into the interior of the country, the United States became the leading agricultural nation in the world. The hardy pioneer farmers produced a vast surplus and emphasis went to producing products with a high-sale value. Such implements as the cotton gin and reaper aided in this. Travel and shipping were greatly assisted in areas not yet touched by railroad or, by improved or new roads, such as the National Road in the East and in the West the Oregon and Santa Fe Trails.

People were exposed to works of literature, art, newspapers, drama, live entertainments, and political rallies. With better communication and travel, more information was desired about previously unknown areas of the country, especially the West. The discovery of gold and other mineral wealth resulted in a literal surge of settlers and even more interest.

Public schools were established in many of the states with more and more children being educated. With more literacy and more participation in literature and the arts, the young nation was developing its own unique culture becoming less and less influenced by and dependent on that of Europe.

More industries and factories required more and more labor. Women, children, and, at times, entire families worked the long hours and days, until the 1830s. By that time, the factories were getting even larger and employers began hiring immigrants who were coming to America in huge numbers. Before then, efforts were made to organize a labor movement to improve working conditions and increase wages. It never really caught on until after the Civil War, but the seed had been sown.

Following is just a partial list of well-known Americans who contributed their leadership and talents in various fields and reforms:

Lucretia Mott and Elizabeth Cady Stanton for **women's rights**

Emma Hart Willard, Catharine Esther Beecher, and Mary Lyon for **education for women**

Dr. Elizabeth Blackwell, the **first woman doctor**

Antoinette Louisa Blackwell, the **first female minister**

Dorothea Lynde Dix for **reforms in prisons and insane asylums**

Elihu Burritt and William Ladd for **peace movements**

Robert Owen for a **Utopian society**

Horace Mann, Henry Barmard, Calvin E. Stowe, Caleb Mills, and John Swett for **public education**

Benjamin Lundy, David Walker, William Lloyd Garrison, Isaac Hooper, Arthur and Lewis Tappan, Theodore Weld, Frederick Douglass, Harriet Tubman, James G. Birney, Henry Highland Garnet, James Forten, Robert Purvis, Harriet Beecher Stowe, Wendell Phillips, and John Brown for **abolition of slavery and the Underground Railroad**

Louisa Mae Alcott, James Fenimore Cooper, Washington Irving, Walt Whitman, Henry David Thoreau, Ralph Waldo Emerson, Herman Melville, Richard Henry Dana,

Nathaniel Hawthorne, Henry Wadsworth Longfellow, John Greenleaf Whittier, Edgar Allan Poe, Oliver Wendell Holmes, **famous writers**

John C. Fremont, Zebulon Pike, Kit Carson, **explorers**

Henry Clay, Daniel Webster, Stephen Douglas, John C. Calhoun, American statemen; Robert Fulton, Cyrus McCormick, Eli Whitney, **inventors**

Noah Webster, American **dictionary and spellers**

The list could go on and on but the contributions of these and many, many others greatly enhanced the unique American culture.

In between the growing economy, expansion westward of the population, and improvements in travel and mass communication, the federal government did face periodic financial depressions. Contributing to these downward spirals were land speculations, availability and soundness of money and currency, failed banks, failing businesses, and unemployment. Sometimes conditions outside the nation would help trigger it; at other times, domestic politics and presidential elections affected it. The growing strength and influence of two major political parties with opposing philosophies and methods of conducting government did not ease matters at times.

As 1860 began, the nation had extended its borders north, south, and west. Industry and agriculture were flourishing. Even though the U.S. did not involve itself actively in European affairs, the relationship with Great Britain was much improved and it and other nations that dealt with the young nation accorded it more respect and admiration. But war was on the horizon. The country was deeply divided along political lines concerning slavery and the election of Abraham Lincoln. Even though 13 colonies won independence, wrote a Constitution forming a union of those states under a central government, fought wars and signed treaties, purchased and explored vast areas of land, developed industry and agriculture, improved transportation, saw population expansion westward, increased each year the number of states admitted to the Union - despite all of these accomplishments, the issue of human slavery had to be settled once and for all. One historian has stated that before 1865, the nation referred to itself as "the United States are . . .," but after 1865, "the United States is . . ." It took the Civil War to finally, completely unify all states into one Union.

6.5 Know the effects of westward expansion

Westward expansion occurred for a number of reasons, one important one being economic. Cotton had become most important to most of the people who lived in the southern states. The effects of the Industrial Revolution, which began in England, were now being felt in the United States. With the invention of power-driven machines, the demand for cotton fiber greatly increased for the yarn needed in spinning and weaving. Eli Whitney's cotton gin made the separation of the seeds from the cotton much more efficient and faster. This, in turn, increased the demand and more and more farmers became involved in the raising and selling of cotton.

The innovations and developments of better methods of long-distance transportation moved the cotton in greater quantities to textile mills in England as well as the areas of New England and Middle Atlantic states in the U.S. As prices increased along with increased demand, southern farmers began expanding by clearing more and more land to grow more cotton. Movement, settlement, and farming headed west to utilize the fertile soils. This, in turn, demanded increased need for a large supply of cheap labor. The system of slavery expanded, both in numbers and in the movement to lands "west" of the South.

Cotton farmers and slave owners were not the only ones heading west.   Many, in other fields of economic endeavor, began the migration: trappers, miners, merchants, ranchers, and others were all seeking their fortunes. The Lewis and Clark expedition stimulated the westward push. Fur companies hired men, known as "Mountain Men", to go westward, searching for the animal pelts to supply the market and meet the demands of the East and Europe. These men in their own way explored and discovered the many passes and trails that would eventually be used by settlers in their trek to the west. The California gold rush also had a very large influence on the movement west.

There were also religious reasons for westward expansion. Increased settlement was encouraged by missionaries who traveled west with the fur traders. They sent word back East for more settlers and the results were tremendous. By the 1840s the population increases in the Oregon country alone were at a rate of about a thousand people a year.   People of many different religions and cultures as well as Southerners with black slaves made their way west which leads to a third reason: political.

It was the belief of many that the United States was destined to control all of the land between the two oceans or as one newspaper editor termed it, "Manifest Destiny." This mass migration westward put the U.S. government on a collision course with the Indians, Great Britain, Spain, and Mexico. The fur traders and missionaries ran up against the Indians in the northwest and the claims of Great Britain for the Oregon country. The U.S. and Britain had shared the Oregon country but by the 1840s, with the increases in the free and slave populations and the demand of the settlers for control and government by the U.S., the conflict had to be resolved. In a treaty, signed in 1846, by both nations, a peaceful resolution occurred with Britain giving up its claims south of the 49th parallel.

In the American southwest, the results were exactly the opposite.   Spain had claimed this area since the 1540s, had spread northward from Mexico City, and, in the 1700s, had established missions, forts, villages and towns, and very large ranches. After the purchase of the Louisiana Territory in 1803, Americans began moving into Spanish territory.   A few hundred American families in what is now Texas were allowed to live there but had to agree to becoming loyal subjects to Spain.   In 1821 Mexico successfully revolted against Spanish rule, won independence, and chose to be more tolerant towards the American settlers and traders. The Mexican government encouraged and allowed extensive trade and settlement, especially in Texas. Many of the new settlers were southerners and brought with them their slaves. Slavery was outlawed in Mexico and technically illegal in Texas, although the Mexican government sort of looked the other way.

With the influx of so many Americans and the liberal policies of the Mexican government, there came to be concern over the possible growth and development of an American state within Mexico.   Settlement restrictions, cancellation of land grants, the forbidding of slavery, and increased military activity brought everything to a head. The order of events include the fight for Texas independence, the brief Republic of Texas, eventual annexation of Texas, statehood, and finally war with Mexico. The Texas controversy was not the sole reason for war. Since American settlers had begun pouring into the Southwest the cultural differences played a prominent part. Language, religion, law, customs, and government were totally different and opposite between the two groups. A clash was bound to occur.

The impact of the entire westward movement resulted in the completion of the borders of the present-day conterminous United States; the bloody war with Mexico; the ever-growing controversy over slave versus free states affecting the balance of power or influence in the U,S.   Congress, especially the Senate; and finally to the Civil War itself.

6.6   Make comparisons of the political, economic, and social characteristics of both North and South from 1800 to 1860

The drafting of the Constitution, its ratification and implementation, united 13 different, independent states into a Union under one central government.   The two crucial compromises of the convention delegates concerning slaves pacified Southerners, especially the slaveowners, but the issue of slavery was not settled and from then on, sectionalism became stronger and more apparent each year putting the entire country on a collision course.

Slavery in the English colonies began in 1619 when 20 Africans arrived in the colony of Virginia at Jamestown. From then on, slavery had a foothold, expecially in the agricultural South, where a large amount of slave labor was needed for the extensive plantations. Free men refused to work for wages on the plantations when land was available for settling on the frontier. So slave labor was the only recourse left. If it had been profitable to use slaves in New England and the Middle Colonies, then without a doubt slavery would have been more widespread. But it came down to whether or not slavery was profitable. It was in the South, but not in the other two colonial regions.

It is interesting that the West was involved in the controversy as well as the North and South. By 1860, the country was made up of these three major regions. The people in all three sections or regions had a number of beliefs and institutions in common. Of course there were major differences with each region having its own unique characteristics. But the basic problem was their development along very different lines.

The section of the North was industrial with towns and factories growing and increasing at a very fast rate. The South had become agricultural, eventually becoming increasingly dependent on the one crop of cotton. In the West, restless pioneers moved into new frontiers seeking land, wealth, and opportunity. Many were from the South and were slaveowners, bringing their slaves with them. So between these three different parts of the country, the views on tariffs, public lands, internal improvements at federal expense, banking and currency, and the issue of slavery were decidedly, totally different. This period of U.S. history is a period of compromises, breakdowns of the compromises, desperate attempts to restore and retain harmony among the three sections, short-lived intervals of the uneasy balance of interests, and ever-increasing conflict.

At the Constitutional Convention, one of the slavery compromises concerned counting slaves for deciding the number of representatives for the House and the amount of taxes to be paid. Southerners pushed for counting the slaves for representation but not for taxes. The Northerners pushed for the opposite. The resulting compromise, sometimes referred to as the "three-fifths compromise," was that both groups agreed that three-fifths of the slaves would be counted for both taxes and representation. The other compromise over slavery was part of the disputes over how much regulation the central government would control over commercial activities such as trade with other nations and the slave trade. It was agreed that Congress would regulate commerce with other nations including taxing imports. Southerners were worried about taxing slaves coming into the country and the possibility of Congress prohibiting the slave trade altogether. The agreement reached allowed the states to continue importation of slaves for the next 20 years until 1808, at which time Congress would make the decision as to the future of the slave trade. During the 20-year period, no more than $10 per person could be levied on slaves coming into the country. These two "slavery" compromises were a necessary concession to have Southern support and approval for the new document and new government. Many Americans felt that the system of slavery would eventually die out in the U.S., but by 1808 cotton was becoming increasingly important in the primarily agricultural South and the institution of slavery had become firmly entrenched in Southern culture. It is also evident that as early as the Constitutional Convention, active anti-slavery feelings and opinions were very strong, leading to extremely active groups and societies.

Democracy is loosely defined as "rule by the people," either directly or through representatives. Associated with the idea of democracy are freedom, equality, and opportunity. The basic concept of democracy existed in the 13 English colonies with the practice of independent self-government. The right of qualified persons to vote, hold office and actively participate in his or her own government is sometimes referred to as "political" democracy. "Social" and "economic" democracy pertain to the idea that all have the opportunity to get an education, choose their own careers, and live as free men everyday all equal in the eyes of the law to everyone. These three concepts of democracy were basic reasons why people came to the New World, and the practices of these concepts continued on through the colonial and revolutionary periods and were extremely influential in the shaping of the new central government under the Constitution. As the nation extended its borders into the lands west of the Mississippi, thousands of settlers streamed into this part of the country bringing with them these ideas and concepts adapting them to the development of the unique characteristics of the region. Equality for everyone, as stated in the Declaration of Independence, did not yet apply to minority groups, black Americans or American Indians. Voting rights and the right to hold public office were restricted in varying degrees in each state. All of these factors decidedly affected the political, economic, and social life of the country and all three were focused in the attitudes of the three sections of the country on slavery.

The first serious clash between North and South occurred during 1819-1820 when James Monroe was in office as President and it was concerning admitting Missouri as a state. In 1819 the U.S. consisted of 21 states: 11 free states and 10 slave states. The Missouri Territory allowed slavery and if admitted would cause an imbalance in the number of U.S. Senators. Alabama had already been admitted as a slave state and that had balanced the Senate with the North and South each having 22 senators. The first Missouri Compromise resolved the conflict by approving admission of Maine as a free state along with Missouri as a slave state, thus continuing to keep a balance of power in the Senate with the same number of free and slave states. An additional provision of this compromise was that with the admission of Missouri, slavery would not be allowed in the rest of the Louisiana Purchase territory north of latitude 36 degrees 30'. This was acceptable to the Southern Congressmen since it was not profitable to grow cotton on land north of this latitude line anyway. It was thought that the crisis had been resolved but in the very next year it was discovered that in its state constitution, Missouri discriminated against the free blacks. Anti-slavery supporters in Congress went into an uproar, determining to exclude Missouri from the Union. Henry Clay, known as the Great Compromiser, then proposed a second Missouri Compromise which was acceptable to everyone. His proposal stated that the Constitution of the United States guaranteed protections and privileges to citizens of states and Missouri's proposed constitution could not deny these to any of its citizens. The acceptance in 1820 of this second compromise opened the way for Missouri's statehood--a temporary reprieve only.

The issue of tariffs also was a divisive factor during this period, especially between 1829 and 1833. The Embargo Act of 1807 and the War of 1812 had completely cut off the source of manufactured goods for Americans, so it was necessary to build factories to produce what was needed. After 1815 when the war had ended, Great Britain proceeded to get rid of its industrial rivals by unloading its goods in America. To protect and encourage its own industries and their products, Congress passed the Tariff of 1816, which required high duties to be levied on manufactured goods coming into the United States. Southern leaders, such as John C. Calhoun of South Carolina, supported the tariff with the assumption that the South would develop its own industries. For a brief period after 1815, the nation enjoyed the "Era of Good Feelings." People were moving into the West; industry and agriculture were growing; a feeling of national pride united Americans in their efforts and determination to strengthen the country. But overspeculation in stocks and lands for quick profits backfired. Cotton prices were rising so many Southerners bought land for cultivation at inflated prices. Manufacturers in the industrial North purchased land to build more plants and factories as an attempt to have a part of this prosperity. Settlers in the West rushed to buy land to reap the benefits of the increasing prices of meat and grain. To have the money for all of these economic activities, all of these groups were borrowing heavily from the banks and the banks themselves encouraged this by giving loans on unsubstantial security.

In late 1818, the Bank of the United States and its branches stopped renewal of personal mortgages and required state banks to immediately pay their bank notes in gold, silver, or in national bank notes. The state banks were unable to do this so they closed their doors and were unable to do any business at all. Since mortgages could not be renewed, people lost all their properties and foreclosures were rampant throughout the country. At the same time, as all of this was occurring, cotton prices collapsed in the English market. Its high prices had caused the British manufacturers to seek cheaper cotton from India for their textile mills. With the fall of cotton prices, the demand for American manufactured goods declined, revealing how fragile the economic prosperity had been. In 1824, a higher tariff was passed by Congress, favoring the financial interests of the manufacturers in New England and the Middle Atlantic states. Also the 1824 tariff was closely tied to the presidential election of that year. Before becoming law, Calhoun had proposed the very high tariffs in an effort to get Eastern business interests to vote with the agricultural interests in the South (who were against it) with supporters of candidate Andrew Jackson siding with whichever side served their best interests. Jackson himself would not be involved in any of this scheming. The bill became law, to Calhoun's surprise, due mainly to the political maneuvering of Martin van Buren and Daniel Webster. By the time the higher 1828 tariff was passed, feelings were extremely bitter in the South, who believed that the New England manufacturers greatly benefitted from it. Vice-President Calhoun, also speaking for his home state of South Carolina, promptly declared that if any state felt that a federal law was unconstitutional, that state could nullify it. In 1832 Congress took the action of lowering the tariffs to a degree but not enough to please South Carolina, which promptly declared the tariff null and void, threatening to secede from the Union. In 1833, Congress lowered the tariffs again, this time at a level acceptable to South Carolina. Even though President Jackson believed in states' rights himself, he also firmly believed in and determined to keep the preservation of the Union. A constitutional crisis had been averted but sectional divisions were getting deeper and more pronounced. The abolition movement was growing rapidly, becoming an important issue in the North.

The slavery issue was at the root of every problem, crisis, event, decision, and struggle from then on. The next crisis involved the issue concerning Texas. By 1836 Texas was an independent republic with its own constitution. During its fight for independence, Americans were sympathetic to and supportive of the Texans and some recruited volunteers crossed into Texas to help the struggle. Problems arose when the state petitioned Congress for statehood. Texas wanted to allow slavery but Northerners in Congress opposed admission to the Union because it would disrupt the balance between free and slave states and give Southerners in Congress increased influence. There were others who believed that granting statehood to Texas would lead to a war with Mexico, which had refused to recognize Texas independence. So for the time being, statehood was put on hold.

Friction increased between land-hungry Americans swarming into western lands and the Mexican government, which controlled these lands. The clash was not only political but cultural and economic. The Spanish influence permeated all parts of southwestern life: law, language, architecture, and customs. By this time the doctrine of Manifest Destiny was in the hearts and on the lips of those seeking new areas of settlement and a new life. Americans were demanding U.S. control of not only the Mexican Territory but also Oregon. Peaceful negotiations with Great Britain secured Oregon but it took two years of war to gain control of the southwestern U.S.

Also, the Mexian government owed debts to U.S. citizens whose property was damaged or destroyed during its struggle for independence from Spain. By the time war broke out in 1845, Mexico had not paid its war debts. The government was weak, corrupt, irresponsible, torn by revolutions, and not in decent financial shape. Mexico was also bitter over American expansion into Texas and the 1836 revolution which resulted in Texas independence. In the 1844 Presidential election, the Democrats pushed for annexation of Texas and Oregon and after winning, they started the procedure to admit Texas to the Union. When statehood occurred, diplomatic relations between the U.S. and Mexico were ended. President Polk wanted U.S. control of the entire southwest, from Texas to the Pacific Ocean. He sent a diplomatic mission with an offer to purchase New Mexico and Upper California but the Mexican government refused to even receive the diplomat. As a result in 1846 of each nation claiming aggression on the part of the other, war was declared. The treaty signed in 1848 and a subsequent one in 1853 completed the southwestern boundary of the United States, reaching to the Pacific Ocean, as President Polk wished.

The slavery issue flared again not to be done away with until the end of the Civil War. It was obvious that the newly acquired territory would be divided up into territories and later become states. In addition to the two factions of Northerners who advocated prohibition of slavery and of Southerners who favored slavery existing there, a third faction arose supporting the doctrine of "popular sovereignty" which stated that people living in territories and states should be allowed to decide for themselves whether or not slavery should be permitted. In 1849 California applied for admittance to the Union and the furor began. The result was the Compromise of 1850, a series of laws designed as a final solution to the issue. Concessions made to the North included the admission of California as a free state and the abolition of slave trading in Washington, D.C. The laws also provided for the creation of the New Mexico and Utah territories. As a concession to Southerners, the residents there would decide whether or not to permit slavery when these two territories became states. Also, Congress authorized implementation of stricter measures to capture runaway slaves.

A few years later, Congress took up consideration of new territories between Missouri and present-day Idaho. Again, heated debate over permitting slavery in these areas flared up. Those opposed to slavery used the Missouri Compromise to prove their point showing that the land being considered for territories was part of the area the Compromise had designated as banned to slavery. But on May 25, 1854, Congress passed the infamous Kansas-Nebraska Act which nullified this provision, created the territories of Kansas and Nebraska, and provided for the people of these two territories to decide for themselves whether or not to permit slavery to exist there. Feelings were so deep and divided that any further attempts to compromise would meet with little, if any, success and political and social turmoil swirled everywhere. Kansas was called "Bleeding Kansas" because of the extreme violence and bloodshed throughout the territory due to the fact that two governments existed there, one pro-slavery and one anti-slavery.

The Supreme Court in 1857 handed down a decision guaranteed to cause explosions throughout the country. Dred Scott was a slave whose owner had taken him from slave state Missouri, then to free state Illinois, into Minnesota Territory, free under the provisions of the Missouri Compromise, then finally back to slave state Missouri. Abolitionists pursued the dilemma by presenting a court case, stating that since Scott had lived in a free state and free territory, he was in actuality a free man. Two lower courts had ruled before the Supreme Court became involved, one ruling in favor and one against. The Supreme Court decided that residing in a free state and free territory did not make Scott a free man because Scott (and all other slaves) were not U.S. citizens or state citizens of Missouri. Therefore, he did not have the right to sue in state or federal courts. The Court went a step further and ruled that the old Missouri Compromise was now unconstitutional due to the fact that Congress did not have the power to prohibit slavery in the Territories

Anti-slavery supporters were stunned. They had just recently formed the new Republican Party and one of its platforms was keeping slavery out of the Territories. Now, according to the decision in the Dred Scott case, this basic party principle was unconstitutional. The only way to ban slavery in new areas was by a Constitutional amendment, requiring ratification by three-fourths of all states. At this time, this was out of the question because the supporters would be unable to get a majority due to Southern opposition.

In 1858 Abraham Lincoln and Stephen A. Douglas were running for the office of U.S. Senator from Illinois and participated in a series of debates which directly affected the outcome of the 1860 Presidential election. Douglas, a Democrat, was up for re-election and knew that if he won this race, he had a good chance of becoming President in 1860. Lincoln, a Republican, was not an abolitionist but he believed that slavery was wrong morally and he firmly believed in and supported the Republican party principle that slavery must not be allowed to be extended any further. Douglas, on the other hand, originated the doctrine of "popular sovereignty" and was responsible for supporting and getting through Congress the inflammatory Kansas-Nebraska Act. In the course of the debates, Lincoln challenged Douglas to show that popular sovereignty reconciled with the Dred Scott decision. Either way he answered Lincoln, Douglas would lose crucial support from one group or the other. If he supported the Dred Scott decision, southerners would support him but he would lose northern support. If he stayed with popular sovereignty, northern support would be his but southern support would be lost. His reply to Lincoln, stating that Territorial legislatures could exclude slavery by refusing to pass laws supporting it, gave him enough support and approval to to be re-elected to the Senate, but it cost him the Democratic nomination for President in 1860. Southerners came to the realization that Douglas may support and be devoted to popular sovereignty but not necessarily to the expansion of slavery. On the other hand, two years later, Lincoln received the nomination of the Republican Party for President.

In 1859 abolitionist John Brown and his followers seized the federal arsenal at Harpers Ferry in what is now West Virginia. His purpose was to take the guns stored in the arsenal, give them to slaves nearby, and lead them in a widespread rebellion. He and his men were captured by Colonel Robert E. Lee of the United States Army and after a trial with a guilty verdict, he was hanged. Most southerners felt that the majority of northerners approved of Brown's action but in actuality, most of them were stunned and shocked. Southern newspapers took great pains to quote a small but well-known minority of abolitionists who applauded and supported Brown's actions. This merely served to widen the gap between the two sections.

The final straw came with the election of Lincoln to the Presidency the next year. Due to a split in the Democratic Party, there were a total of four candidates from four political parties. With Lincoln receiving a minority of the popular vote and a majority of electoral votes, the Southern states, one by one, voted to secede from the Union as they had promised they would do if Lincoln and the Republicans were victorious. The die was cast.

6.7 Be knowledgeable about the Civil War and Reconstruction from 1860 to 1877

It is ironic that South Carolina was the first state to secede from the Union and the first shots of the war were fired on Fort Sumter in Charleston Harbor. Both sides quickly made preparations for war. The North had more in its favor: a larger population; superiority in finances and transportation facilities; manufacturing, agricultural, and natural resources. The North possessed most of the nation's gold, had about 92% of all industries, and almost all known supplies of copper, coal, iron, and various other minerals. Since most of the nation's railroads were in the North and mid-West, men and supplies could be moved wherever needed; food could be transported from the farms of the mid-West to workers in the East and to soldiers on the battlefields. Trade with nations overseas could go on as usual due to control of the navy and the merchant fleet. The Northern states numbered 24 and included western (California and Oregon) and border (Maryland, Delaware, Kentucky, Missouri, and West Virginia) states.

The Southern states numbered 11 and included South Carolina, Georgia, Florida, Alabama, Mississippi, Louisiana, Texas, Virginia, North Carolina, Tennessee, and Arkansas, making up the Confederacy. Even though outnumbered in population, the South was completely confident of victory. They knew that all they had to do was fight a defensive war, protecting their own territory until the North, who had to invade and defeat an area almost the size of Western Europe, tired of the struggle and gave up. Another advantage of the South was that a number of its best officers had graduated from the U.S. Military Academy at West Point and had had long years of army experience, some even exercising varying degrees of command in the Indian wars and the war with Mexico. Men from the South were conditioned to living outdoors and were more familiar with horses and firearms than many men from Northeastern cities. Since cotton was such an important crop, Southerners felt that British and French textile mills were so dependent on raw cotton that they would be forced to help the Confederacy in the war. The South had specific reasons and goals for fighting the war, moreso than the North. The major aim of the Confederacy never wavered: to win independence, the right to govern themselves as they wished, and to preserve slavery. The Northerners were not as clear in their reasons for conducting war. At the beginning, most believed, along with Lincoln, that preservation of the Union was paramount. Only a few extremely fanatical abolitionists looked on the war as a way to end slavery once and for all. However, by war's end, more and more northerners had come to believe that freeing the slaves was just as important as restoring the Union.

The war strategies for both sides were relatively clear and simple.   The South planned a defensive war, wearing down the North until it agreed to peace on southern terms. The only exception was to gain control of Washington, D.C., go north through the Shenandoah Valley into Maryland and Pennsylvania in order to drive a wedge between the Northeast and mid-West, interrupt the lines of communication, and end the war quickly. The North had three basic strategies:

(1) blockade the Confederate coastline in order to cripple the South

(2) seize control of the Mississippi River and interior railroad lines to split the Confederacy in two

(3) seize the Confederate capital of Richmond, Virginia, driving southward joining up with Union forces coming east from the Mississippi Valley.

The South won decisively until the Battle of Gettysburg, July 1 - 3, 1863. Until Gettysburg, Lincoln's commanders, McDowell and McClellan, were less than desirable; Burnside and Hooker, not what was needed. Lee, on the other hand, had many able officers, Jackson and Stuart depended on heavily by him. Jackson died at Chancellorsville and was replaced by Longstreet. Lee decided to invade the North and depended on J.E.B. Stuart and his cavalry to keep him informed of the location of Union troops and their strengths. Four things worked against Lee at Gettysburg:

(1) the Union troops gained the best positions and the best ground first, making it easier to make a stand there.

(2) Lee's move into Northern territory put him and his army a long way from food and supply lines. They were more or less on their own.

(3) Lee thought that his Army of Northern Virginia was invincible and could fight and win under any conditions or circumstances.

Consequently he made the mistake of failing to listen to Longstreet and following the strategy of regrouping back into Southern territory to the supply lines. Lee felt that regrouping was retreating and almost an admission of defeat. He was convinced the army would be victorious. Longstreet was concerned about the Union troops occupying the best positions and felt that regrouping to a better position would be an advantage. He was also very concerned about the distance from supply lines.

(4) Stuart and his men did not arrive at Gettysburg until the end of the second day of fighting and by then, it was too little too late. He and the men had had to detour around Union soldiers and he was delayed getting the information Lee needed.

It was not the intention of either side to fight there but the fighting began when a Confederate brigade stumbled into a unit of Union cavalry while looking for shoes. The third and last day Lee launched the final attempt to break Union lines. General George Pickett sent his division of three brigades under Generals Garnet, Kemper, and Armistead against Union troops on Cemetary Ridge under command of General Winfield Scott Hancock. Union lines held and Lee and the defeated Army of Northern Virginia made their way back to Virginia. Although Lincoln's commander George Meade successfully turned back a Confederate charge, he and the Union troops failed to pursue Lee and the Confederates. This battle was the turning point for the North. After this, Lee never again had the troop strength to launch a major offensive.

The day after Gettysburg, on July 4th, Vicksburg, Mississippi, surrendered to Union General Ulysses Grant, thus severing the western Confederacy from the eastern part. In September 1863, the Confederacy won its last important victory at Chickamauga. In November the Union victory at Chattanooga made it possible for Union troops to go into Alabama and Georgia, splitting the eastern Confederacy in two. Lincoln gave Grant command of all Northern armies in March of 1864. Grant led his armies into battles in Virginia while Phil Sheridan and his cavalry did as much damage as possible. In a skirmish at a place called Yellow Tavern, Virginia, Sheridan's and Stuart's forces met, with Stuart being fatally wounded. The Union won the Battle of Mobile Bay and in May 1864 William Tecumseh Sherman began his march to successfully demolish Atlanta, then on to Savannah. He and his troops turned northward through the Carolinas to Grant in Virginia. On April 9, 1865, Lee formally surrendered to Grant at Appamattox Courthouse, Virginia.

The Civil War took more American lives than any other war in history, the South losing one-third of its soldiers in battle compared to about one-sixth for the North. More than half of the total deaths were caused by disease and the horrendous conditions of field hospitals. Both sections paid a tremendous economic price but the South suffered more severely from direct damages. Destruction was pervasive with towns, farms, trade, industry, lives and homes of men, women, children all destroyed and an entire Southern way of life was lost. The deep resentment, bitterness, and hatred that remained for generations gradually lessened as the years went by but legacies of it surface and remain to this day. The South had no voice in the political, social, and cultural affairs of the nation, lessening to a great degree the influence of the more traditional Southern ideals. The Northern Yankee Protestant ideals of hard work, education, and economic freedom became the standard of the United States and helped influence the development of the nation into a modern, industrial power.

SOCIAL SCIENCE HIGH SCHOOL

The effects of the Civil War were tremendous. It changed the methods of waging war and has been called the first modern war. It introduced weapons and tactics that, when improved later, were used extensively in wars of the late 1800s and 1900s. Civil War soldiers were the first to fight in trenches, first to fight under a unified command, first to wage a defense called "major cordon defense", a strategy of advance on all fronts. They were also the first to use repeating and breechloading weapons. Observation balloons were first used during the war along with submarines, ironclad ships, and mines. Telegraphy and railroads were put to use first in the Civil War. It was considered a modern war because of the vast destruction and was "total war", involving the use of all resources of the opposing sides. There was probably no way it could have ended other than total defeat and unconditional surrender of one side or the other.

By executive proclamation and constitutional amendment, slavery was officially and finally ended, although there remained deep prejudice and racism, still raising its ugly head today. But also, the Union was preserved and the states were finally truly united. Sectionalism, especially in the area of politics, remained strong for another 100 years but not to the degree and with the violence as existed before 1861. It has been noted that the Civil War may have been American democracy's greatest failure for, from 1861 to 1865, calm reason, basic to democracy, fell to human passion. Yet, democracy did survive. The victory of the North established once and for all that no state has the right to end or leave the Union. As a result of unity, the U.S. became a major global power. Lincoln never purposed to punish the South. He was most concerned with restoring the South to the Union in a program that was flexible and practical rather than rigid and unbending. In fact he never really felt that the states had succeeded in leaving the Union but that they had left the "family circle" for a short time. His plans consisted of two major steps:

(1) All southerners taking an oath of allegiance to the Union promising to accept all federal laws and proclamations dealing with slavery would receive a full pardon. The only ones excluded from this were men who had resigned from civil and military positions in the federal government to serve in the Confederacy, those who were part of the Confederate government, those in the Confederate army above the rank of lieutenant, and Confederates who were guilty of mistreating prisoners of war and blacks.

(2) A state would be able to write a new constitution, elect new officials, and return to the Union fully equal to all other states on certain conditions: a minimum number of persons (at least 10% of those who were qualified voters in their states before secession from the Union who had voted in the 1860 election) must take an oath of allegiance.

As the war dragged on to its bloody, destructive conclusion, Lincoln was very concerned and anxious to get the states restored to the Union and showed flexibility in his thinking as he made changes to his Reconstruction program to make it as easy and painless as possible. Of course, Congress had final approval of many actions and it would be interesting to know how differently things might have turned out if Lincoln had lived to see some or all of his kind policies, supported by fellow moderates, put into action. But, unfortunately, it didn't turn out that way. After Andrew Johnson became President and the radical Republicans gained control of Congress, the harsh measures of radical Reconstruction were implemented.

The economic and social chaos in the South after the war was unbelievable with starvation and disease rampant, especially in the cities. The U.S. Army provided some relief of food and clothing for both white and blacks but the major responsibility fell to the Freedmen's Bureau. Though the bureau agents to a certain extent helped southern whites, their main responsibility was to the freed slaves. They were to assist the freedmen to become self-supporting and protect them from being taken advantage of by others. Northerners looked on it as a real, honest effort to help the South out of the chaos it was in. Most white Southerners charged the bureau with causing racial friction, deliberately encouraging the freedmen to consider former owners as enemies. As a result, as southern leaders began to be able to restore life as it had once been, they adopted a set of laws known as "black codes", containing many of the provisions of the prewar "slave codes." There were certain improvements in the lives of freedmen, but, basically, the codes denied the freedmen their basic civil rights. In short, except for the condition of freedom and a few civil rights, white southerners made every effort to keep the freedmen in a way of life subordinate to theirs.

Radicals in Congress pointed out these illegal actions by white Southerners as evidence that they were unwilling to recognize, accept, and support the complete freedom of black Americans and could not be trusted. So Congress drafted its own program of Reconstruction, including laws that would protect and further the rights of blacks. Three amendments were added to the Constitution: the 13th Amendment of 1865 outlawed slavery throughout the entire United States. The 14th Amendment of 1868 made blacks American citizens. The 15th Amendment of 1870 gave black Americans the right to vote and made it illegal to deny anyone the right to vote on the basis of race.

Federal troops were stationed throughout the South and protected Republicans who took control of southern governments. Bitterly resentful, white Southerners fought the new political system by joining a secret society called the Ku Klux Klan, using violence to keep black Americans from voting and getting equality. But before being allowed to rejoin the Union, the Confederate states were required to agree to all federal laws. Between 1866 and 1870, all of them had returned to the Union, but Northern interest in Reconstruction was fading. Reconstruction officially ended when the last Federal troops left the South in 1877. It can be said that Reconstruction had a limited success as it set up public school systems and expanded legal rights of black Americans. But white supremacy came to be in control once again and its bitter fruitage is still with us today.

Lincoln and Johnson had considered the conflict of Civil War as a "rebellion of individuals," but Congressional Radicals, such as Charles Sumner in the Senate, considered the southern states as complete political organizations and were now in the same position as any unorganized Territory and should be treated as such. Radical House leader Thaddeus Stevens considered the Confederate States, not as Territories, but as conquered provinces and felt they should be treated that way. President Johnson refused to work with Congressional moderates, insisting on having his own way. As a result, the Radicals gained control of both houses of Congress and when Johnson opposed their harsh measures, they came within one vote of impeaching him. General Grant was elected President in 1868, serving two scandal-ridden terms. He was himself an honest, upright person but he greatly lacked political experience and his greatest weakness was a blind loyalty to his friends. He absolutely refused to believe that his friends were not honest and stubbornly would not admit to their using him to further their own interests. One of the sad results of the war was the rapid growth of business and industry with large corporations controlled by unscrupulous men. But after 1877, some degree of normalcy returned and there was time for rebuilding, expansion, and growth.

6.8 Understand the significance of post-Reconstruction industrialization and reform

There was a marked degree of industrialization before and during the Civil War, but at war's end, industry in America was small. After the war, dramatic changes took place: machines replacing hand labor, extensive nationwide railroad service making possible the wider distribution of goods, invention of new products made available in large quantities, large amounts of money from bankers and investors for expansion of business operations. American life was definitely affected by this phenomenal industrial growth. Cities became the centers of this new business activity resulting in mass population movements there and tremendous growth. This new boom in business resulted in huge fortunes for some Americans and extreme poverty for many others. The discontent this caused resulted in a number of new reform movements from which came measures controlling the power and size of big business and helping the poor. Of course, industry before, during, and after the Civil War was centered mainly in the North, especially the tremendous industrial growth after. The late 1800s and early 1900s saw the increasing buildup of military strength and the U.S. becoming a world power.

The use of machines in industry enabled workers to produce a large quantity of goods much faster than by hand. With the increase in business, hundreds of workers were hired, assigned to perform a certain job in the production process. This was a method of organization called "division of labor" and by its increasing the rate of production, businesses lowered prices for their products making the products affordable for more people. As a result, sales and businesses were increasingly successful and profitable.

A great variety of new products or inventions became available such as: the typewriter, the telephone, barbed wire, the electric light, the phonograph, and the gasoline automobile. From this list the one that had the greatest effect on America's economy was the automobile.

The increase in business and industry was greatly affected by the many rich natural resources that were found throughout the nation. The industrial machines were powered by the abundant water supply. The construction industry as well as products made from wood depended heavily on lumber from the forests. Coal and iron ore in abundance were needed for the steel industry which profited and increased from the use of steel in such things as skyscrapers, automobiles, bridges, railroad tracks, and machines. Other minerals such as silver, copper, and petroleum played a large role in industrial growth, especially petroleum, from which gasoline was refined as fuel for the increasingly popular automobile.

Between 1870 and 1916, more than 25 million immigrants came into the United States adding to the phenomenal population growth taking place. This tremendous growth aided business and industry in two ways: (1) The number of consumers increased creating a greater demand for products thus enlarging the markets for the products. And (2) with increased production and expanding business, more workers were available for newly created jobs. The completion of the nation's transcontinental railroad in 1869 contributed greatly to the nation's economic and industrial growth. Some examples of the benefits of using the railroads include: raw materials were shipped quickly by the mining companies and finished products were sent to all parts of the country. Many wealthy industrialistes and railroad owners saw tremendous profits steadily increasing due to this improved method of transportation.

As business grew, methods of sales and promotion were developed. Salespersons went to all parts of the country, promoting the varied products, opening large department stores in the growing cities, offering the varied products at reasonable affordable prices. People who lived too far from the cities, making it impossible to shop there, had the advantage of using a mail order service, buying what they needed from catalogs furnished by the companies. The developments in communication, such as the telephone and telegraph, increased the efficiency and prosperity of big business.

Investments in corporate stocks and bonds resulted from business prosperity. As individuals began investing heavily in an eager desire to share in the profits, their investments made available the needed capital for companies to expand their

operations. From this, banks increased in number throughout the country, making loans to businesses and significant contributions to economic growth. At the same time, during the 1880s, government made little effort to regulate businesses. This gave rise to monopolies where larger businesses got rid of their smaller competitors and assumed complete control of their industries. Some owners in the same business would join or merge to form one company. Others formed what were called "trusts," a type of monopoly in which rival businesses were controlled but not formally owned. Monopolies had some good effects on the economy. Out of them grew the large, efficient corporations which made important contributions to the growth of the nation's economy. Also, the monopolies enabled businesses to keep their sales steady and avoid sharp fluctuations in price and production. At the same time, the downside of monopolies was the unfair business practices of the business leaders. Some acquired so much power that they took unfair advantage of others. Those who had little or no competition would require their suppliers to supply goods at a low cost, sell the finished products at high prices, and reduce the quality of the product to save money.

The late 1800s and early 1900s were a period of the efforts of many to make significant reforms and changes in the areas of politics, society, and the economy. There was a need to reduce the levels of poverty and to improve the living conditions of those affected by it. Regulations of big business, getting rid of governmental corruption and making it more responsive to the needs of the people were also on the list of reforms to be accomplished. Until 1890, there was very little success, but from 1890 on, the reformers gained increased public support and were able to achieve some influence in government. Since some of these individuals referred to themselves as "progressives," the time period of 1890 to 1917 is referred to by historians as the Progressive Era.

Skilled laborers were organized into a labor union called the American Federation of Labor, in an effort to gain better working conditions and wages for its members. Farmers joined organizations such as the National Grange and Farmers Alliances. Farmers were producing more food than people could afford to buy, the result of (1) new farm lands rapidly opening up on the plains and prairies, and (2) development and availability of new farm machinery and newer and better methods of farming. They tried selling their surplus abroad but faced stiff competition from other nations selling the same farm products. Other problems contributed significantly to their situation. Items they needed for daily life were priced exorbitantly high. Having to borrow money to carry on farming activities kept them constantly in debt. Higher interest rates, shortage of money, falling farm prices, having to deal with the so-called middlemen, and the increasingly high charges by the railroads to haul farm products to large markets all contributed to the desperate need for reform to relieve the plight of American farmers.

American women began actively campaigning for the right to vote. Elizabeth Cady Stanton and Susan B. Anthony in 1869 founded the organization called National Women Suffrage Association, the same year the Wyoming Territory gave women the right to vote. Soon after, a few states followed by giving women the right to vote, limited to local elections only.

Governmental reform began with the passage of the Civil Service Act, also known as the Pendleton Act. It provided for the Civil Service Commission, a federal agency responsible for giving jobs based on merit rather than as political rewards or favors. Another successful reform was the adoption of the secret ballot in voting, as were such measures as the direct primary, referendum, recall, and direct election of U.S. Senators by the people rather than by their state legislatures. Following the success of reforms made at the national level, the progressives were successful in gaining reforms in government at state and local levels.

After 1890, more and more attention was called to needs and problems through the efforts of social workers and clergy and the writings of people such as Lincoln Steffans, Ida M. Tarbell, and Upton Sinclair. Presidents Theodore Roosevelt, William Howard Taft, and Woodrow Wilson supported many of the reform laws after 1890 and in 1884, President Grover Cleveland did much to see that the Civil Service Act was enforced. After 1880, a number of political or "third" parties were formed and although unsuccessful in getting their Presidential candidates elected, significant reform legislation, including Constitutional amendments, were passed by Congress and became law due to their efforts. Such legislative acts included the Sherman Antitrust Act of 1890, the Clayton Antitrust Act of 1914, the Underwood Tariff of 1913, and the establishment of the Federal Trade Commission in 1914. By the 1890s and early 1900s, the United States had become a world power and began a leading role in international affairs. War loomed on the horizon once again and the stage was set for increased activity in world affairs which had been avoided since the end of the Civil War.

6.9 Understand the importance and impact of events, issues, and effects of the period of World War I

During the time period of 1823 to the 1890s, the major interests and efforts of the American people were concentrated on expansion, settlement, and development of the continental United States. The Civil War, 1861-1865, preserved the Union and eliminated the system of slavery and from 1865 onward, the focus was on taming the West and developing industry. During this period of time, travel and trade between the United States and Europe were continuous. By the 1890s, American interests turned to areas outside the boundaries of the United States. The West was developing into a major industrial area and people in the United States became very interested in selling their factory and farm surplus to overseas markets. In fact, some Americans desired getting and controlling land outside the U.S. boundaries. Before the 1890s, the U.S. had little, if anything, to do with foreign affairs, was not a strong nation militarily, and had inconsequential influence on international political affairs. In fact, the Europeans looked on the American diplomats as inept and bungling in their diplomatic efforts and activities. But all of this changed and the Spanish-American War of 1898 saw the entry of the United States as a world power.

During the 1890s, Spain controlled such overseas possessions as Puerto Rico, the Philippines, and Cuba. Cubans rebelled against Spanish rulership and the U.S. government found itself beseiged by demands from Americans to assist the Cubans in their revolt. When the U.S. battleship Maine blew up off the coast of Havana, Cuba, Americans blamed the Spaniards for it and demanded American action against Spain. Two months later, Congress declared war on Spain and the U.S. quickly defeated them. The peace treaty gave the U.S. possession of Puerto Rico, the Philippines, Guam and Hawaii which was annexed during the war.

This success enlarged and expanded the U.S. role in foreign affairs. Under the administration of Theodore Roosevelt, the U.S. armed forces were built up, greatly increasing its strength. Roosevelt's foreign policy was summed up in the slogan of "Speak softly and carry a big stick," backing up the efforts in diplomacy with a strong military. During the years before the outbreak of World War I, evidence of U.S. emergence as a world power could be seen in a number of actions. Using the Monroe Doctrine of non-involvement of Europe in the affairs of the Western Hemisphere, President Roosevelt forced Italy, Germany, and Great Britain to remove their blockade of Venezuela; gained the rights to construct the Panama Canal by threatening force; assumed the finances of the Dominican Republic to stabilize it and prevent any intervention by Europeans; and in 1916 under President Woodrow Wilson, to keep order, U.S. troops were sent to the Dominican Republic.

In Europe, war broke out in 1914 and ended in 1918, eventually involving nearly 30 nations. One of the major causes of the war was the tremendous surge of nationalism during the 1800s and early 1900s. People of the same nationality or ethnic group sharing a common history, language or culture began uniting or demanding the right of unification, especially in the empires of eastern Europe, such as Russia, Ottoman and Austrian-Hungarian Empires. Getting stronger and more intense were the beliefs of these peoples in loyalty to common political, social, and economic goals, considered to be before any loyalty to the controlling nation or empire. Emotions ran high and minor disputes magnified into major ones and sometimes quickly led to threats of war. Especially sensitive to these conditions was the area of the states on the Balkan Peninsula. Along with the imperialistic colonization for industrial raw materials, military build-up (especially by Germany), and diplomatic and military alliances, the conditions for one tiny spark to set off the explosion were in place. In July 1914, a Serbian national assassinated the Austrian heir to the throne and his wife and war began a few weeks later. There were a few attempts to keep war from starting, but these efforts were futile.

World War I saw the introduction of such warfare as use of tanks, airplanes, machine guns, submarines, poison gas, and flame throwers. Fighting on the Western front was characterized by a series of trenches which were used throughout the war until 1918. U.S. involvement in the war did not occur until 1916. When it began in 1914, President Woodrow Wilson declared that the U.S. was neutral and most Americans were opposed to any involvement anyway. In 1916, Wilson was reelected to a second term on the basis of the slogan proclaiming his efforts at keeping America out of the war. For a few months after, he put forth most of his efforts to stopping the war but German submarines began unlimited warfare against American merchant shipping. At the same time, Great Britain intercepted and decoded a secret message from Germany to Mexico urging Mexico to go to war against the U.S. The publishing of this information along with continued German destruction of American ships resulted in the eventual entry of the U.S. into the conflict, the first time the country prepared to fight in a conflict not on American soil. Though unprepared for war, governmental efforts and activities resulted in massive defense mobilization with America's economy directed to the war effort. Though America made important contributions of war materials, its greatest contribution to the war was manpower--soldiers desperately needed by the Allies.

Some ten months before the war ended, President Wilson had proposed a program called the Fourteen Points as a method of bringing the war to an end with an equitable peace settlement. In these Points he had five points setting out general ideals; there were eight pertaining to immediately working to resolve territorial and political problems; and the fourteenth point counseled establishing an organization of nations to help keep world peace. When Germany agreed in 1918 to an armistice, it assumed that the peace settlement would be drawn up on the basis of these Fourteen Points. But the peace conference in Paris basically ignored these points and Wilson had to be content with efforts at establishing the League of Nations. Italy, France, and Great Britain, having suffered and sacrificed far more in the war than America, wanted retribution. The treaties punished severely the Central Powers, taking away arms and territories and requiring payment of reparations. Germany was punished more than the others and, according to one clause in the treaty, was forced to assume the responsibility for causing the war.

Pre-war empires lost tremendous amounts of territories as well as the wealth of natural resources in them. New, independent nations were formed and some predominately ethnic areas came under control of nations of different cultural backgrounds. Some national boundary changes overlapped and created tensions and hard feelings as well as political and economic confusion. The wishes and desires of every national or cultural group could not possibly be realized and satisfied, resulting in disappointments for both those who were victorious and those who were defeated. Germany received harsher terms than expected from the treaty which weakened its post-war government and, along with the world-wide depression of the 1930s, set the stage for the rise of Adolf Hitler and his Nationalist Socialist Party and World War II.

President Wilson lost in his efforts to get the U.S. Senate to approve the peace treaty. The Senate at the time was a reflection of American public opinion and its rejection of the treaty was a rejection of Wilson. The approval of the treaty would have made the U.S. a member of the League of Nations but Americans had just come off a bloody war to ensure that democracy would exist throughout the world. Americans just did not want to accept any responsibility that resulted from its new position of power and were afraid that membership in the League of Nations would embroil the U.S. in future disputes in Europe.

6.10 Understand the importance and impact of events, issues, and effects of the period of World War II

The end of World War I and the decade of the 1920s saw tremendous changes in the United States, signifying the beginning of its development into its modern society today. The shift from farm to city life was occurring in tremendous numbers. Social changes and problems were occurring at such a fast pace that it was extremely difficult and perplexing for many Americans to adjust to them. Politically the 18th Amendment to the Consitution, the so-called prohibition amendment, prohibited selling alcoholic beverages throughout the U.S. resulting in problems affecting all aspects of society. The passage of the 19th Amendment gave to women the right to vote in all elections. The decade of the 1920s also showed a marked change in roles and opportunities for women with more and more of them seeking and finding careers outside the home. They began to think of themselves as the equal of men and not as much as housewives and mothers.

The influence of the automobile, the entertainment industry, and the rejection of the morals and values of pre-World War I life, resulting in the fast-paced "Roaring Twenties", had significant effects on events leading to the depression-era 1930s and another world war. Many Americans greatly desired the pre-war life and supported political policies and candidates in favor of the return to what was considered to be normal. It was desired to end government's strong role and adopt a policy of isolating the country from world affairs, a result of the war.

Prohibition of the sale of alcohol had caused the increased activities of bootlegging and the rise of underworld gangs and the illegal speakeasies, the jazz music and dances they promoted. The customers of these clubs were considered "modern," reflected by extremes in clothing, hair styles, and attitudes towards authority and life. Movies and, to a certain degree, other types of entertainment, along with increased interest in sports figures and the accomplishments of national heroes, such as Lindbergh, influenced Americans to admire, emulate, and support individual accomplishments. As wild and uninhibited modern behavior became, this decade witnessed an increase in a religious tradition known as "revivalism," emotional preaching. Even though law and order were demanded by many Americans, the administration of President Warren G. Harding was marked by widespread corruption and scandal, not unlike the administration of Ulysses S. Grant, except Grant was honest and innocent. The decade of the 20s also saw the resurgence of such racist organizations as the Ku Klux Klan.

The U.S. economy experienced a tremendous period of boom. Restrictions on business because of war no longer existed and the conservatives in control adopted policies that helped and encouraged big business. To keep foreign goods from competing with American goods, tariffs were raised to the highest level. New products were developed by American manufacturers and many different items became readily available to the people. These included refrigerators, radios, washing machines, and, most importantly, the automobile.

Americans in the 1920s heavily invested in corporation stocks, providing companies a large amount of capital for expanding their businesses. The more money investors put into the stock market, the more the value of the stocks increased. This, in turn, led to widespread speculation which increased stock value to a point beyond the level that was justified by earnings and dividends. Much of the stock speculation involved paying a small part of the cost and borrowing the rest. This led eventually to the stock market crash of 1929, financial ruin for many investors, a weakening of the nation's economy, and the Great Depression of the 1930s. The depression hit the United States tremendously hard resulting in bank failures, loss of jobs due to cut-backs in production, and a lack of money leading to a sharp decline in spending which in turn affected business, factories and stores, and higher unemployment. Farm products were not affordable so the farmers suffered even more. Foreign trade sharply decreased and in the early 1930s, the U.S. economy was effectively paralyzed. Europe was affected even more so.

The war had seriously damaged the economies of the European countries, both the victors and the defeated, leaving them deeply in debt. There was difficulty on both sides paying off war debts and loans. It was difficult to find jobs and some countries like Japan and Italy found themselves with not enough resources and more than enough people. Solving these problems by expanding territorially merely set up conditions for war later. Germany suffered horribly with runaway inflation ruining the value of its money and wiping out the savings of millions. Even though the U.S. made loans to Germany, which helped the government to restore some order and which provided a short existence of some economic stability in Europe, the Great Depression only served to undo any good that had been done. Mass unemployment, poverty, and despair greatly weakened the democratic governments that had been formed and greatly strengthened the increasing power and influence of extreme political movements, such as communism, fascism, and national socialism, which promised to put an end to the economic problems.

The extreme form of patriotism called nationalism that had been the chief cause of World War I grew even stronger after the war ended in 1918. The political, social, and economic unrest fueled nationalism and it became an effective tool enabling dictators to gain and maintain power from the 1930s to the end of World War II in 1945. In the Soviet Union, Joseph Stalin succceeded in gaining political control and establishing a strong harsh dictatorship. Benito Mussolini and the Fascist party, promising prosperity and order in Italy, gained national support and set up a strong government. n Japan, even though the ruler was considered to be **Emperor Hirohito**, actual control and administration of government came under military officers. In Germany, the results of war, harsh treaty terms, loss of territory, great economic chaos and collapse all enabled **Adolf Hitler** and his Nazi party to gain complete power and control.

Germany, Italy, and Japan initiated a policy of aggressive territorial expansion with Japan being the first to conquer. In 1931 the Japanese forces seized control of Manchuria, a part of China containing rich natural resources, and in 1937 began an attack on China, occupying most of its eastern part by 1938. Italy invaded Ethiopia in Africa in 1935, having it totally under its control by 1936. The Soviet Union did not invade or take over any territory but along with Italy and Gremany, actively participated in the Spanish Civil War, using it as a proving ground to test tactics and weapons setting the stage for World War II.

In Germany, almost immediately after taking power, in direct violation of the World War I peace treaty, Hitler began the buildup of the armed forces. He sent troops into the Rhineland in 1936, invaded Austria in 1938 and united it with Germany, seized control of the Sudetenland in 1938 (part of western Czechoslovakia and containing mostly Germans), the rest of Czechoslovakia in March 1939, and, on September 1, 1939, began World War II in Europe by invading Poland. In 1940 Germany invaded and controlled Norway, Denmark, Belgium, Luxembourg, the Netherlands, and France.

After the war began in Europe, U.S. **President Franklin D. Roosevelt** announced that the United States was neutral. Most Americans, although hoping for an Allied victory, wanted the U.S. to stay out of the war. President Roosevelt and his supporters, called "interventionists," favored all aid except war to the Allied nations fighting Axis aggression. They were fearful that an Axis victory would seriously threaten and endanger all democracies. On the other hand, the "isolationists" were against any U.S. aid being given to the warring nations, accusing President Roosevelt of leading the U.S. into a war very unprepared to fight. Roosevelt's plan was to defeat the Axis nations by sending the Allied nations the equipment needed to fight: ships, aircraft, tanks, and other war materials.

In Asia, the U.S. had opposed Japan's invasion of Southeast Asia, an effort to gain Japanese control of that region's rich resources. As a result, the U.S. stopped all important exports to Japan, whose industries depended heavily on petroleum, scrap metal, and other raw materials. Later Roosevelt refused the Japanese withdrawal of its funds from American banks. General Tojo became the Japanese premier in October 1941 and quickly realized that the U.S. Navy was powerful enough to block Japanese expansion into Asia. Deciding to cripple the Pacific Fleet, the Japanese aircraft, without warning, bombed the Fleet December 7, 1941, while at anchor in **Pearl Harbor** in Hawaii. Temporarily it was a success. It destroyed many aircraft and disabled much of the U.S. Pacific Fleet. But, in the end, it was a costly mistake as it quickly motivated the Americans to prepare for and wage war.

Military strategy in the European theater of war as developed by **Roosevelt, Churchill, and Stalin** was to concentrate on Germany's defeat first, then Japan's. The start was made in North Africa, pushing Germans and Italians off the continent, beginning in the summer of 1942 and ending successfully in May 1943. Before the war, Hitler and Stalin had signed a nonaggression pact in 1939 which Hitler violated in 1941 by invading the Soviet Union. The German defeat at Stalingrad, marking a turning point in the war, was brought about by a combination of entrapment by Soviet troops and death of German troops by starvation and freezing due to the horrendous winter conditions. All of this occurred at the same time the Allies were driving them out of North Africa. The liberation of Italy began in July 1943 and ended May 2, 1945. The third part of the strategy was **D-Day, June 6, 1944,** with the Allied invasion of France at Normandy. At the same time, starting in January 1943, the Soviets began pushing the German troops back into Europe and they were greatly assisted by supplies from Britain and the United States. By April 1945, Allies occupied positions beyond the Rhine and the Soviets moved on to Berlin, surrounding it by April 25th. Germany surrendered May 7th and the war in Europe was finally over.

Meanwhile, in the Pacific, in the six months after the attack on Pearl Harbor, Japanese forces moved across Southeast Asia and the western Pacific Ocean. By August 1942, the Japanese Empire was at its largest size and stretched northeast to Alaska's Aleutian Islands, west to Burma, south to what is now Indonesia. Invaded and controlled areas included Hong Kong, Guam, Wake, Thailand, part of Malaysia, Singapore, the Philippines, and bombed Darwin on the north coast of Australia. The raid of General Doolittle's bombers on Japanese cities and the American naval victory at Midway along with the fighting in the Battle of the Coral Sea helped turn the tide against Japan. Island-hopping by U.S. Seabees and Marines and the grueling bloody battles fought resulted in gradually pushing the Japanese back towards Japan. After victory was attained in Europe, concentrated efforts were made to secure Japan's surrender, but it took dropping two atomic bombs on the cities of Hiroshima and Nagasaki to finally end the war in the Pacific. Japan formally surrendered on September 2, 1945, aboard the U.S. battleship Missouri, anchored in Tokyo Bay. The war was finally ended.

Before war in Europe had ended, the Allies had agreed on a military occupation of Germany, with it being divided into four zones each one occupied by Great Britain, France, the Soviet Union, and the United States and the four powers jointly administering Berlin. After the war, the Allies agreed that Germany's armed forces would be abolished, the Nazi Party outlawed, and the territory east of the Oder and Neisse Rivers taken away. Nazi leaders were accused of war crimes and brought to trial. After Japan's defeat, the Allies began a military occupation directed by American General Douglas MacArthur, who introduced a number of reforms eventually ridding Japan of its military institutions transforming it into a democracy. A constitution was drawn up in 1947 transferring all political rights from the emperor to the people, granting women the right to vote, and denying Japan the right to declare war. War crimes trials of 25 war leaders and government officials were also conducted. The U.S. did not sign a peace treaty until 1951. The treaty permitted Japan to rearm but took away its overseas empire.

Again, after a major world war came efforts to prevent war from occurring again throughout the world. Preliminary work began in 1943 when the U.S., Great Britain, the Soviet Union, and China sent representatives to Moscow where they agreed to set up an international organization that would work to promote peace around the earth. In 1944, the **four Allied powers** met again and made the decision to name the organization the United Nations. In 1945 a charter for the U.N. was drawn up and signed, taking effect in October of that year.

Major consequences of the war included horrendous death and destruction, millions of displaced persons, the gaining of strength and spread of Communisn and Cold War tensions as a result of the beginning of the nuclear age. World War II ended more lives and caused more devastation than any other war. Besides the losses of millions of military personnel, the devastation and destruction directly affected civilians, reducing cities, houses, and factories to ruin and rubble and totally wrecking communication and transportation systems. Millions of civilian deaths, especially in China and the Soviet Union, were the **results of famine**.

More than 12 million people were uprooted by wars end having no place to live. Included were prisoners of war, those who survived Nazi concentration camps and slave labor camps, orphans, and people who escaped war-torn areas and invading armies. Changing national boundary lines also caused the mass movement of displaced persons.

Germany and Japan were completely defeated; Great Britain and France were seriously weakened; and the Soviet Union and the United States became the world's leading powers. Although allied during the war, the alliance fell apart as the Soviets pushed Communism in Europe and Asia. In spite of the tremendous destruction it suffered, the Soviet Union was stronger than ever. During the war, it took control of Lithuania, Estonia, and Latvia and by mid-1945 parts of Poland, Czechoslovakia, Finland, and Romania. It helped Communist governments gain power in Bulgaria, Romania, Hungary, Czechoslovakia, Poland, and North Korea. China fell to **Mao Zedong's** Communist forces in 1949. Until the fall of the Berlin Wall in 1989 and the dissolution of Communist governments in Eastern Europe and the Soviet Union, the United States and the Soviet Union faced off in what was called a Cold War, with the possibility of the terrifying destruction by nuclear weapons a likely deterrent to nuclear war.

6.11 Know and understand the key events and issues pertaining to foreign affairs from post-World War II to the present

The major thrust of U.S. foreign policy from the end of World War II to 1990 was the post-war struggle between non-Communist nations, led by the United States, and the Soviet Union and the Communist nations who were its allies. It was referred to as a "Cold War" because its conflicts did not lead to a major war of fighting, or a "hot war." Both the Soviet Union and the United States embarked on an arsenal buildup of atomic and hydrogen bombs as well as other nuclear weapons. Both nations had the capability of destroying each other but because of the continuous threat of nuclear war and accidents, extreme caution was practiced on both sides. The efforts of both sides to serve and protect their political philosophies and to support and assist their allies resulted in a number of events during this 45-year period.

In 1946 Josef Stalin stated publicly that the presence of capitalism and its development of the world's economy made international peace impossible. This resulted in an American diplomat in Moscow named George F. Kennan to propose, as a response to Stalin and as a statement of U.S. foreign policy, the idea and goal of the U.S. to be to contain or limit the extension or expansion of Soviet Communist policies and activities. After Soviet efforts to make trouble in Iran, Greece, and Turkey, U.S. President Harry Truman stated what is known as the Truman Doctrine which committed the U.S. to a policy of intervention in order to contain or stop the spread of communism throughtout the world.

After 1945, social and economic chaos continued in Western Europe, especially in Germany. Secretary of State George C. Marshall came to realize that the U.S. had greatly underestimated how extensive the war damage and resulting chaos had been. To avoid further serious problems and to assist in the recovery, he proposed a program known as the European Recovery Program or the Marshall Plan. Although the Soviet Union withdrew from any participation, the U.S. continued the work of assisting Europe in regaining economic stability. In Germany the situation was critical with the American Army shouldering the staggering burden of relieving the serious problems of the German economy. In February 1948 Britain and the U.S. combined their two zones, with France joining in June. The Soviets were opposed to German unification and in April 1948 took serious action to either stop it or to force the Allies to give up control of West Berlin to the Soviets. The Soviets blocked all road traffic access to West Berlin from West Germany. To avoid any armed conflict, it was decided to airlift into West Berlin the needed food and supplies. From June 1948 to mid-May 1949 Allied air forces flew in all that was needed for the West Berliners, forcing the Soviets to lift the blockade and permit vehicular traffic access to the city.

The first "hot war" in the post-World War II era was the Korean War, begun June 25, 1950 and ending July 27, 1953. Troops from Communist North Korea invaded democratic South Korea in an effort to unite both sections under Communist control.

The United Nations organization asked its member nations to furnish troops to help restore peace. Many nations responded and President Truman sent American troops to help the South Koreans. The war dragged on for three years and ended with a truce, not a peace treaty. Like Germany then, Korea remained divided and does so to this day.

In 1954, the French were forced to give up their colonial claims in Indochina, the present-day countries of Vietnam, Laos, and Cambodia. Afterwards, the Communist northern part of Vietnam began battling with the democratic southern part over control of the entire country. In the late 1950s and early 1960s, U.S. Presidents Eisenhower and Kennedy sent to Vietnam a number of military advisers and military aid to assist and support South Vietnam's non-Communist government. During Lyndon Johnson's presidency, the war escalated with thousands of American troops being sent to participate in combat with the South Vietnamese. The war was extremely unpopular in America and caused such serious divisiveness among its citizens that Johnson decided not to seek reelection in 1968. It was in President Richard Nixon's second term in office that the U.S. signed an agreement ending war in Vietnam and restoring peace. This was done January 27, 1973, and by March 29th, the last American combat troops and American prisoners of war left Vietnam for home. It was the longest war in U.S. history and to this day carries the perception that it was a "lost war."

In 1962 during the administration of President John F. Kennedy, Premier Khrushchev and the Soviets decided, as a protective measure for Cuba against an American invasion, to install nuclear missiles on the island. In October, American U-2 spy planes photographed over Cuba what were identified as missile bases under construction. The decision in the White House was how to handle the situation without starting a war. The only recourse was removal of the missile sites and preventing more being set up. Kennedy announced that the U.S. had set up a "quarantine" of Soviet ships heading to Cuba. It was in reality a blockade but the word itself could not be used publicly as a blockade was actually considered an act of war. A week of incredible tension and anxiety gripped the entire world until Khrushchev capitulated. Soviet ships carrying missiles for the Cuban bases turned back and the crisis eased. What precipitated the crisis was Khrushchev's unerestimation of Kennedy. The President made no effort to prevent the erection of the Berlin Wall and was reluctant to commit American troops to invade Cuba and overthrow Fidel Castro. The Soviets assumed this was a weakness and decided they could install the missiles without any interference.

The Soviets were concerned about American missiles installed in Turkey aimed at the Soviet Union and about a possible invasion of Cuba. If successful, Khrushchev would demonstrate to the Russian and Chinese critics of his policy of peaceful coexistence that he was tough and not to be intimidated. At the same time, the Americans feared that if Russian missiles were put in place and launched from Cuba to the U.S., the short distance of 90 miles would not give enough time for adequate warning and be coming from a direction radar systems didn't cover. Also, it was felt that if America gave in and allowed a Soviet presence practically at the back door that the effect on American security and morale would be devastating. As tensions eased in the aftermath of the crisis, several agreements were made. The missiles in Turkey were removed. as actually they were obsolete. A telephone "hot line" was set up between Moscow and Washington to make it possible for the two heads of government to have instant contact with each other. The U.S. agreed to sell its surplus wheat to the Soviets.

Probably the highlight of the foreign policy of President Richard Nixon, after the ending of the Vietnam War and withdrawal of troops, was his 1972 trip to China. Since 1949, when the Communists gained control of China, the policy of the U.S. government was refusal to recognize the Communist government but to regard as the legitimate government of China to be that of Chiang Kai-shek, exiled on the island of Taiwan. In 1971, Nixon sent Henry Kissinger on a secret trip to Peking to investigate whether or not it would be possible for America to give recognition to China. In February 1972 President and Mrs. Nixon spent a number of days in the country visiting well-known Chinese landmarks, dining with the two leaders, Mao Tse-tung and Chou En-lai. Agreements were made for cultural and scientific exchanges, eventual resumption of trade, and future unification of the mainland wirh Taiwan. In 1979 formal diplomatic recognition was achieved. With this one visit, the pattern of the Cold War was essentially shifted.

In the administration of **President Jimmy Carter**, **Egyptian President Anwar el-Sadat** and **Israeli Prime Minister Menachem Begin** met at presidential retreat **Camp David** and agreed, after a series of meetings, to sign a formal treaty of peace between the two countries. In 1979, the Soviet invasion of Afghanistan was perceived by Carter and his advisers as a threat to the rich oil fields in the Persian Gulf but at the time, U.S. military capability to prevent further Soviet aggression in the Middle East was weak. The last year of Carter's presidential term was taken up with the 53 American hostages held in Iran. The shah had been deposed and control of the government and the country was in the hands of Muslim leader, **Ayatollah Ruhollah Khomeini**. Khomeini's extreme hatred for the U.S. was the result of the 1953 overthrow of Iran's Mossadegh government, sponsored by the CIA. To make matters worse, the CIA proceeded to train the shah's ruthless secret police force. So when the terminally ill exiled shah was allowed into the U.S. for medical treatment, a fanatical mob stormed into the American embassy taking the 53 Americans as prisoners, supported and encouraged by Khomeini. President Carter froze all Iranian assets in the U.S., set up trade restrictions, and approved a risky rescue attempt which failed. He had appealed to the UN for aid in gaining release for the hostages and to European allies to join the trade embargo on Iran. Khomeini ignored UN requests for releasing the Americans and Europeans refused to support the embargo so as not to risk losing access to Iran's oil. American prestige was damaged and Carter's chances for reelection were doomed. The hostages were released on the day of Ronald Reagan's inauguration as President when Carter released Iranian assets as ransom.

The foreign policy of **President Ronald Reagan** was, in his first term, focused primarily on the Western Hemisphere, particularly in Central America and the West Indies. U.S. involvement in the domestic revolutions of El Salvador and Nicaragua continued into Reagan's second term when Congress held televised hearings on what came to be known as the Iran-Contra Affair. A cover-up was exposed showing that profits from secretly selling military hardware to Iran had been used to give support to rebels, called Contras, who were fighting in Nicaragua. In 1983 in Lebanon, 241 American Marines were killed when an Islamic suicide bomber drove an explosive-laden truck into U.S. Marines headquarters located at the airport in Beirut. This tragic event came as part of the unrest and violence between the Israelis and PLO forces in southern Lebanon. In the same month, 1,900 U.S. Marines landed on the island of Grenada to rescue a small group of American medical students at the medical school and depose the leftist government. But perhaps the most intriguing and far-reaching event towards the end of Reagan's second term was the arms-reduction agreement Reagan reached with **Soviet General Secretary Mikhail Gorbachev**. Gorbachev began easing East-West tensions by stressing the importance of cooperation with the West and easing the harsh and restrictive life of the people in the Soviet Union. In retrospect, it was clearly a prelude to the events occurring during the administration of **President George Bush**.

After Bush took office, it appeared for a brief period that democracy would gain a hold and influence in China but the brief movement was quickly and decisively crushed. The biggest surprise was the fall of the Berlin Wall, resulting in the unification of all of Germany, the loss of power of the Communists in other Eastern European countries, and the fall of Communism in the Soviet Union and the breakup of its republics into independent nations. The countries of Poland, Hungary, Romania, Czechoslovakia, Albania, and Bulgaria replaced Communist rule for a democratic one. The former Yugoslavia broke apart into individual ethnic enclaves with the republics of Serbia, Croatia, and Bosnia-Hercegovina embarking on wars of ethnic cleansing between Catholics, Orthodox, and Muslims. In Russia, as in the other former republics and satellites, democratic governments were put into operation and the difficult task of changing communist economies into ones of capitalistic free enterprise began. For all practical purposes, it appeared that the tensions and dangers of the post-World War II "Cold War" between the U.S. and Soviet-led Communism were over.

President Bush, in December of 1989, sent U.S. troops to invade Panama and arrest the **Panamanian dictator Manuel Noriega**. Although he had periodically assisted CIA operations with intelligence information, at the same time, Noriega laundered money from drug smuggling and gunrunning through Panama's banks. Though ignored for a short time, it became too embarassing for the American intelligence community. When a political associate tried unsuccessfully to depose him and an off-duty U.S. Marine was shot and killed at a roadblock, Bush took action. Noriega was brought to the U.S. where he stood trial on charges of drug distribution and racketeering.

During the time of the American hostage crisis, Iraq and Iran fought a war in which the U.S. and most of Iraq's neignbors supported Iraq. In a five-year period, **Saddam Hussein** received from the U.S. $500 million worth of American technology, including lasers, advanced computers, and special machine tools used in missile development. The Iraq-Iran war was a bloody one resulting in a stalemate with a UN truce ending it. Neighboring Kuwait, in direct opposition to OPEC agreements, increased oil production. This caused oil prices to drop which upset Hussein, who was deeply in debt from the war and totally dependent on oil revenues. After a short period of time, Saddam invaded and occupied Kuwait. The U.S. made extensive plans to put into operation strategy to successfully carry out Operation Desert Storm, the liberation of Kuwait. In four days, February 24-28, 1991, the war was over and Iraq had been defeated, its troops driven back into their country. Saddam remained in power even though Iraq's economy was seriously damaged.

President Bill Clinton sent U.S. troops to Haiti to protect the efforts of Jean-Bertrand Aristide to gain democratic power and to Bosnia to assist UN peacekeeping forces. He also inherited from the Bush administration the problem of Somalia in East Africa, where U.S. troops had been sent in December 1992 to support UN efforts to end the starvation of the Somalis and restore peace. The efforts were successful at first but eventually failed due to the severity of the intricate political problems within the country. After U.S. soldiers were killed in an ambush along with 300 Somalis, American troops were withdrawn and returned home.

6.12 Recognize and be able to discuss the political, economic, and social issues of the 20th century

During the late 1800s and early 1900s, many Americans were concerned about and began actively campaigning for significant changes and reforms in the social, economic, and political systems in the country. Among their goals were ridding government of corruption, regulating big businesses, reducing poverty, improving the lives of the poor and their living conditions, and ensuring more government response to the needs of the people.

Early efforts at reforms began with movements to organize farmers and laborers, the push to give women the right to vote, and the successful passage of Congressional legislation establishing merit as the basis for federal jobs rather than political favoritism. Other efforts were directed towards improvements in education, living conditions in city slums, breaking up trusts and monopolies in big businesses.

After World War I ended, the 18th Amendment to the U.S. Constitution was passed, forbidding the sale of alcoholic beverages. The violence and upheaval it caused was a major characteristic of the wild decade of the 1920s. The wild financial speculations came to an abrupt end with the stock market crash of October 1929 plunging the U.S. into the Great Depression.

The election of Franklin Roosevelt to the office of President in 1932 was the start of the social and economic recovery and reform legislative acts designed to gradually ease the country back to more prosperity. These acts included relief for the nation's farmers, regulation of banks, public works providing jobs for the unemployed, and giving aid to manufacturers. Some of the agencies set up to implement these measures included the Works Progress Administration (WPA), Civilian Conservation Camps (CCC), the Farm Credit Administration (FCA), and the Social Security Board. These last two agencies gave credit to farmers and set up the nation's social security system.

After World War II and the Korean War, efforts began to relieve the problems of millions of African-Americans, including ending discrimination in education, housing, and jobs and ending the grinding widespread poverty. The efforts of civil rights leaders found success in a number of Supreme Court decisions, the best-known case, "Brown vs Board of Education of Topeka (1954)" ending compulsory segregation in public schools. In the 1960s, the civil rights movement under the leadership of **Dr. Martin Luther King, Jr.**, really gained momentum and under **President Lyndon B. Johnson**, the **Civil Rights Acts of 1964 and 1968** prohibited discrimination in housing sales and rentals, employment, public accomodations, and voter registration.

Poverty remained a serious problem in the central sections of large cities resulting in riots and soaring crime rates which ultimately found its way to the suburbs. The escalation of the war in Vietnam and the social conflict and upheaval of support vs opposition to U.S. involvement led to antiwar demonstrations, escalation of drug abuse, weakening of the family unit, homelessness, poverty, mental illness, along with increasing social, mental, and physical problems experienced by the Vietnam veterans returning to families, marriages, and a country all divided and torn apart.

The Watergate scandal resulting in the first-ever resignation of a sitting American president was the most crucial domestic crisis of the 1970s. The population of the U.S. had greatly increased and along with it the nation's industries and the resulting harmful pollution of the environment. Factory smoke, automobile exhaust, waste from factories and other sources all combined to create hazardous air, water, and ground pollution which, if not brought under control and significantly diminished, would severely endanger all life on earth. The 1980s was the decade of the horrible Exxon Valdez oil spill off the Alaskan coast and the nuclear accident and melt-down at the Ukrainian nuclear power plant at Chernobyl. The U.S. had a close call with the near disaster at Three Mile Island Nuclear Plant in Pennsylvania.

Inflation increased in the late 1960s, and the 1970s witnessed a period of high unemployment, the result of a severe recession. The decision of the OPEC (Organization of Petroleum Exporting Countries) ministers to cut back on oil production thus raising the price of a barrel of oil created a fuel shortage. This made it clear that energy and fuel conservation was a must in the American economy, especially since fuel shortages created two energy crises in the decade of the 70s. Americans experienced shortages of fuel oil for heating and gasoline for cars and other vehicles.

The 1980s saw the ups and downs of rising inflation, recession, recovery, and the insecurity of long-term employment. Foreign competition and imports, the use of robots and other advanced technology in industries, the opening and operation of American companies and factories in other countries to lower labor costs all contributed to the economic and employment problems. The nation's farmers experienced economic hardships and October 1987 saw another one day significant drop in the Dow Jones on the New York Stock Exchange. January 28, 1986 was the day of the loss of the seven crew members of the NASA space shuttle "Challenger". The reliability and soundness of numerous savings and loans institutions were in serious jeopardy when hundreds of these failed and others went into bankruptcy due to customer default on loans and mismanagement. Congressional legislation helped rebuild the industry.

6.13 Recognize the significant accomplishments made by immigrant, racial, ethnic, and gender groups

Most students of American history are aware of the tremendous influx of immigrants to America during the 19th century. It is also a known fact that the majority settled in the ethnic neighborhoods and communities of the large cities, close to friends, relatives, and the work they were able to find. But there is one interesting fact some are not aware of and that is, after the U.S. Congress passed the 1862 Homestead Act, when the Civil War ended and the West began to open up for settlement, more than half of the hardy pioneers who went to homestead and farm western lands were European immigrants: Swedes, Norwegians, Czechs, Germans, Danes, Finns, and Russians.

But, by far, the nation's immigrants were an important reason for America's phenomenol industrial growth from 1865 to 1900. They came seeking work and better opportunities for themselves and their families than what life in their native country could give them. What they found in America was suspicion and distrust because they were competitors with Americans for jobs, housing, and decent wages. Their languages, customs, and ways of living were different, especially between the different national and ethnic groups. Until the early 1880s most immigrants were from the parts of northwestern Europe such as Germany, Scandinavia, the Netherlands, Ireland, and Great Britain. After 1890 the new arrivals increasingly came from eastern and southern Europe. Chinese immigrants on the Pacific coast, so crucial to the construction of the western part of the first transcontinental railroad, were the first to experience this increasing distrust which eventually erupted into violence and bloodshed. From about 1879 to the present time, the U.S. Congress made, repealed, and amended numerous pieces of legislation concerning quotas, restrictions, and other requirements pertaining to immigrants. The immigrant laborers, both skilled and unskilled, were the foundation of the modern labor union movement as a means of gaining recognition, support, respect, rights, fair wages, and better working conditions.

The historical record of African-Americans is known to all. Sold into slavery by rival tribes, they were brought against their will to the West Indies and southern America to slave on the plantations in a life-long condition of servitude and bondage. The 13th Constitutional Amendment abolished slavery; the 14th gave them U.S. citizenship; and the 15th gave them the right to vote. Efforts of well-known African-Americans resulted in some improvements although the struggle was continuous without let-up. Many were outspoken and urged and led protests against the continuing onslaught of discrimination and inequality. The leading black spokesman from 1890 to 1915 was educator Booker T. Washington. He recognized the need of vocational education for African-Americans, educating them for skills and training for such areas as domestic service, farming, the skilled trades, and small business enterprises. He founded and built in Alabama the famous Tuskegee Institute.

W.E.B. DuBois, another outstanding African-American leader and spokesman, believed that only continuous and vigorous protests against injustices and inequalities coupled with appeals to black pride would effect changes. The results of his efforts was the formation of the Urban League and the NAACP (the National Association for the Advancement of Colored People) which today continue to eliminate discriminations and secure equality and equal rights. Others who made significant contributions were **Dr. George Washington Carver's** work improving agricultural techniques for both black and white farmers; the writers William Wells Brown, Paul L. Dunbar, Langston Hughes, and Charles W. Chesnutt; the music of Duke Ellington, W.C. Handy, Marion Anderson, Louis Armstrong, Leontyne Price, Jessye Norman, Ella Fitzgerald, and many, many others.

Students of American history are greatly familiar with the accomplishments and contributions of American women. Previous mention has been made of the accomplishments of such 19th century women as: writer Louisa Mae Alcott; abolitionist Harriet Beecher Stowe; women's rights activists Elizabeth Cady Stanton and Lucretia Mott; physician Dr. Elizabeth Blackwell; women's education activists Mary Lyon, Catharine Esther Beecher, and Emma Hart Willard; prison and asylum reform activist Dorothea Dix; social reformer, humanitarian, pursuer of peace Jane Addams; aviatrix Amelia Earhart; women's suffrage activists Susan B. Anthony, Carrie Chapman Catt,

and Anna Howard Shaw; Supreme Court Associate Justices Sandra Day O'Connor and Ruth Bader Ginsberg; and many, many more who have made tremendous contributions in science, politics and government, music and the arts (such as Jane Alexander who is National Chairperson of the National Endowment for the Arts), education, athletics, law, etc.

Bibliography

Adams, James Truslow (1965). "The March of Democracy," Vol 1. "The Rise of the Union". New York: Charles Scribner's Sons, Publisher.

Barbini, John & Warshaw, Steven, (1985). "The World Past and Present." New York: Harcourt, Brace, Jovanovich, Publishers.

Berthon, Simon & Robinson, Andrew. (1991). "The Shape of the World." Chicago: Rand McNally, Publisher.

Bice, David A. (1989). "A Panorama of Florida II". (Second Edition). Marceline, Missouri: Walsworth Publishing Co., Inc.

Bram, Leon (Vice-President and Editorial Director)(1983). "Funk and Wagnalls New Encyclopedia." United States of America.

Burns, Edward McNall & Ralph, Philip Lee. (1974). "World Civilizations Their History and Culture" (5th ed.). New York: W.W. Norton & Company, Inc., Publishers.

Dauben, Joseph W. (1990). "The World Book Encyclopedia." Chicago: World Book Inc. A Scott Fetzer Company, Publisher.

De Blij, H.J. & Muller, Peter O. (1991). "Geography Regions and Concepts" (Sixth Edition). New York: John Wiley & Sons, Inc., Publisher.

Encyclopedia Americana. (1985). Danbury, Connecticut: Grolier Incorporated, Publisher.

Heigh, Christopher. (Editor)(1985). "The Cambridge Historical Encyclopedia of Great Britain and Ireland." Cambridge: Cambridge University Press, Publisher.

Hunkins, Francis P. & Armstrong, David G. (1984). "World Geography People and Places." Columbus, Ohio: Charles E. Merrill Publishing Co. A Bell & Howell Company, Publishers.

Jarolimek, John; Anderson, J. Hubert & Durand, Loyal, Jr. (1985). "World Neighbors." New York: Macmillan Publishing Company. London: Collier Macmillan Publishers.

McConnell, Campbell R. (1987). "Economics-Principles, Problems, and Policies" (Tenth Edition). New York: McGraw-Hill Book Company, Publisher.

Millard, Dr. Anne & Vanags, Patricia. (1985). "The Usborne Book of World History." London: Usborne Publishing Ltd., Publisher.

SOCIAL SCIENCE HIGH SCHOOL

Novosad, Charles (Executive Editor)(1994). "The Nystrom Desk Atlas." Chicago: Nystrom Division of Herff Jones, Inc., Publisher.

Patton, Clyde P.; Rengert, Arlene C.; Saveland, Robert N.; Cooper, Kenneth S. & Caro, Patricia T. (1985). "A World View." Morristown, N.J.: Silver Burdette Company, Publisher.

Schwartz, Melvin & O'Connor, John R. (1984). "Exploring A Changing World." New York: Globe Book Company, Publisher.

"The Annals of America: Selected Readings on Great Issues in American History 1620-1968." (1969). United States of America: William Benton, Publisher.

Tindall, George Brown & Shi, David E. (1996). "America-A Narrative History" (Fourth Edition). New York: W.W. Norton & Company, Publisher.

Todd, Lewis Paul & Curti, Merle. (1972). "Rise of the American Nation" (Third Edition). New York: Harcourt, Brace, Jovanovich, Inc., Publishers.

Tyler, Jenny; Watts, Lisa; Bowyer, Carol; Trundle, Roma & Warrender, Annabelle (1984) "The Usborne Book of World Geography." London: Usborne Publishing Ltd., Publisher.

Willson, David H. (1972). "A History of England." Hinsdale, Illinois: The Dryden Press, Inc., Publisher.

DIRECTIONS: Read each item and select the best response.

1. **Which one of the following is not a reason why Europeans came to the New World?**

   A. To find resources in order to increase wealth.

   B. To establish trade

   C. To increase a ruler's power and importance.

   D. To spread Christianity.

2. **The study of human origins has been a major contribution of**

   A. Evans

   B. Schliemann

   C. Margaret Mead

   D. The Leakeys

3. **Downstream for the flow of the Yangtze River is primarily**

   A. North

   B. South

   C. East

   D. West

4. **The results of the Renaissance, Enlightenment, Commercial and Industrial Revolutions were more unfortunate for the people of**

   A. Asia

   B. Latin America

   C. Africa

   D. Middle East

5. **Government regulation of economic activities for favorable balance of trade was the first major economic theory. It was called**

   A. Laissez-faire

   B. Globalism

   C. Mercantilism

   D. Syndicalism

6. **The first ancient civilization to introduce and practice monotheism was the**

   A. Sumerians

   B. Minoans

   C. Phoenicians

   D. Hebrews

7. **Which one of the following is not a responsibility of citizens?**

   A. Pay taxes
   B. Defend the country
   C. Obey the laws
   D. Serve on juries

8. **Which one of the following does not affect climate?**

   A. Elevation or altitude
   B. Ocean currents
   C. Latitude
   D. Longitude

9. **The foundation of modern constitutionalism is embodied in the idea that government is limited by law. This was stated by**

   A. John Locke
   B. Rousseau
   C. St. Thomas Aquinas
   D. Montesquieu

10. **The only colony not founded and settled for religious, political, or business reasons was**

    A. Delaware
    B. Virginia
    C. Georgia
    D. New York

11. **The "father of political science" is considered to be**

    A. Aristotle
    B. John Locke
    C. Plato
    D. Thomas Hobbes

12. **Bathtubs, hot and cold running water, and sewage systems with flush toilets were developed by the**

    A. Minoans
    B. Mycenaeans
    C. Phoenicians
    D. Greeks

13. In the Low countries of Western Europe, the achievements of the Renaissance were unsurpassed and made these countries outstanding cultural centers on the continent. This was accomplished because of

    A. Foreign domination
    B. The establishment of universities
    C. The printing of some of the first books
    D. Wealth and trade connections with southern Europe

14. Of the thirteen English colonies, the greatest degree of religious toleration was found in

    A. Maryland
    B. Rhode Island
    C. Pennsylvania
    D. Delaware

15. The chemical process of radiocarbon dating would be most useful and beneficial in the field of

    A. Archaeology
    B. Geography
    C. Sociology
    D. Anthropology

16. Which one of the following is not an important legacy of the Byzantine Empire?

    A. It protected Western Europe from various attacks from the east by such groups as the Persians, Ottoman Turks, and Barbarians
    B. It played a part in preserving the literature, philosophy, and language of ancient Greece
    C. Its military organization was the foundation for modern armies
    D. It kept the legal traditions of Roman government, collecting and organizing many ancient Roman laws

17. In the United States, federal investigations into business activities are handled by the

    A. Department of Treasury
    B. Security and Exchange Commission
    C. Government Accounting Office
    D. Federal Trade Commission

18. The makeup of today's modern newspapers - including comics, puzzles, sports, columnists - was a technique first used by

    A. William Randolph Hearst
    B. Edward W. Scripps
    C. Joseph Pulitzer
    D. Charles A. Dana

19. **The Renaissance philosopher who wrote that there was no hatred that was so absolute as that which was Christian was**

    A. Rabelais

    B. Erasmus

    C. Montaigne

    D. Bacon

20. **The most important Civil War battle fought in Florida was the Confederate victory at**

    A. Fort Pickens

    B. Olustee

    C. Fort Clinch

    D. Cedar Key

21. **Downstream for the flow of the Nile is**

    A. North

    B. South

    C. East

    D. West

22. **The year 1619 was a memorable year for the colony of Virginia. Three important events occurred resulting in lasting effects on U.S. history. Which one of the following was not one of the events?**

    A. Twenty African slaves arrived.

    B. The London Company granted the colony a charter making it independent.

    C. The colonists were given the right by the London Company to govern themselves through representative government in the Virginia House of Burgesses.

    D. The London Company sent to the colony 60 women who were quickly married, establishing families and stability in the colony.

23. **Of all of the major causes of both World Wars I and II, the most significant one is considered to be**

    A. Extreme nationalism

    B. Military buildup and aggression

    C. Political unrest

    D. Agreements and alliances

24. **The end to hunting, gathering, and fishing of prehistoric people was due to**

    A. Domestication of animals

    B. Building crude huts and houses

    C. Development of agriculture

    D. Organized government in villages

25. **In the United States government, power or control over public education, marriage, and divorce is**

    A. Implied or suggested

    B. Concurrent or shared

    C. Delegated or expressed

    D. Reserved

26. **The principle of "popular sovereignty" allowing people in any Territory to make their own decision concerning slavery was stated by**

    A. Henry Clay

    B. Daniel Webster

    C. John C. Calhoun

    D. Stephen A. Douglas

27. **Under the brand new Constitution, the most urgent of the many problems facing the new federal government was that of**

    A. Maintaining a strong army and navy

    B. Establishing a strong foreign policy

    C. Raising money to pay salaries and war debts

    D. Setting up courts, passing federal laws, and providing for law enforcement officers

28. **Which one of the following was not a reason why the United States went to war with Great Britain in 1812?**

Resentment by Spain over the sale, exploration, and settlement of the Louisiana Territory

The westward movement of farmers because of the need for more land

Canadian fur traders were agitating the northwestern Indians to fight American expansion

Britain continued to seize American ships on the high seas and force American seamen to serve aboard British ships

29. Which one of the following is not a reason for Florida's rapid growth during the 1880s?

A. Extensive road building

B. Draining swamplands

C. Discovery of large deposits of phosphate

D. Influx of people and money into the state

30. "Participant observation" is a method of study most closely associated with and used in

A. Anthropology

B. Archaeology

C. Sociology

D. Political science

31. The early ancient civilizations developed systems of government

A. To provide for defense against attack

B. To regulate trade

C. To regulate and direct the economic activities of the people as they worked together in groups

D. To decide on the boundaries of the different fields during planting seasons

32. The "divine right" of kings was the key political characteristic of

A. The Age of Absolutism

B. The Age of Reason

C. The Age of Feudalism

D. The Age of Despotism

33. The principle of zero in mathematics is the discovery of the ancient civilization found in

A. Egypt

B. Persia

C. India

D. Babylon

34. The Ganges River empties into the

A. Bay of Bengal

B. Arabian Sea

C. Red Sea

D. Arafura Sea

35. One South American country quickly and easily gained independence in the 19th century from European control; was noted for the uniqueness of its political stability and gradual orderly changes. This most unusual Latin American country is

   A. Chile

   B. Argentina

   C. Venezuela

   D. Brazil

36. Surveying is described as a technique of measurement used to determine the position of points and boundaries. Which one of the following would not have any need or reason to use surveyors in field studies and research?

   A. Sociology

   B. Geography

   C. Archaeology

   D. History

37. U.S. foreign minister Robert R. Livingstone said, "From this day the United States take their place among the greatest powers." He was referring to the action taken by President Thomas Jefferson

   A. Who had authorized the purchase of the Louisiana Territory

   B. Who sent the U.S. Marines and naval ships to fight the Barbary pirates

   C. Who had commissioned the Lewis and Clark expedition

   D. Who repealed the Embargo Act

38. The only Central American country with no standing army, a freely elected government, and considered the oldest democracy in the region is

   A. Costa Rica

   B. Belize

   C. Honduras

   D. Guatemala

39. During the 1920s, the United States almost completely stopped all immigration. One of the reasons was

   A. Plentiful cheap unskilled labor was no longer needed by industrialists

   B. War debts from World War I made it difficult to render financial assistance

   C. European nations were reluctant to allow people to leave since there was a need to rebuild populations and economic stability

   D. The United States did not become a member of the League of Nations

40. 1763 was the year of Great Britain's total victory over her European rivals and the establishment of a global empire. Of the American colonies, a European statesman accurately prophesied that these colonies no longer needed English protection and would soon gain independence. He was

   A. Edmund Burke

   B. Comte de Rochambeau

   C. Count Vergennes

   D. William Pitt

41. Colonial expansion by Western European powers in the 18th and 19th centuries was due primarily to

   A. Building and opening the Suez Canal

   B. The Industrial Revolution

   C. Marked improvements in transportation

   D. Complete independence of all the Americas and loss of European domination and influence

42. America's weak foreign policy and lack of adequate diplomacy during the 1870s and 1880's led to the comment that "a special Providence takes care of fools, drunkards, and the United States" is attributed to

   A. Otto von Bismarck

   B. Benjamin Disraeli

   C. William Gladstone

   D. Paul von Hindenburg

43. It can reasonably be stated that the change in the United States from primarily an agricultural country into a giant industrial power was due to a great degree to

   A. Tariffs on foreign imports

   B. Millions of hard-working immigrants

   C. An increase in technological developments

   D. The change from steam to electricity for powering industrial machinery

44. Many American authors were noted for "local-color" writings about the way of life in certain regions. Which one of the following was not associated with the other three in writing about life in the mining camps of the west?

   A. Hamlin Garland

   B. Joaquin Miller

   C. Bret Harte

   D. Mark Twain

45. There is no doubt of the vast improvement of the U.S. Constitution over the weak Articles of Confederation. Which one of the four accurate statements below is a unique yet eloquent description of the document?

   A. The establishment of a strong central government in no way lessened or weakened the individual states.

   B. Individual rights were protected and secured.

   C. The Constitution is the best representation of the results of the American genius for compromise.

   D. Its flexibility and adaptation to change gives it a sense of timelessness.

46. The study of a people's language and writing would be part of all of the following except

   A. Sociology

   B. Archaeology

   C. History

   D. Geography

47. The changing focus during the Renaissance when artists and scholars were less concerned with religion but centered their efforts on a better understanding of people and the world was called

A. Realism

B. Humanism

C. Individualism

D. Intellectualism

48. The "father of anatomy" is considered to be

A. Vesalius

B. Servetus

C. Galen

D. Harvey

49. In the United States government, the power of coining money is

A. Implied or suggested

B. Concurrent or shared

C. Delegated or expressed

D. Reserved

50. The source of authority for national, state, and local governments in the U.S. is

A. The will of the people

B. The U.S. Constitution

C. Written laws

D. The Bill of Rights

51. India's greatest ruler is considered to be

A. Akbar

B. Asoka

C. Babur

D. Jahan

52. "Poverty is the parent of revolution and crime" was from the writings of

A. Plato

B. Aristotle

C. Cicero

D. Gaius

53. Geography was first studied in an organized manner by

A. The Egyptians

B. The Greeks

C. The Romans

D. The Arabs

54. From about 1870 to 1900 the settlement of America's "last frontier", the West, was completed. One attraction for settlers was free land but it would have been to no avail without

A. Better farming methods and technology

B. Surveying to set boundaries

C. Immigrants and others to seek new land

D. The railroad to get them there

55. Meridians, or lines of longitude, not only help in pinpointing locations but are also used for

A. Measuring distance from the Poles

B. Determining direction of ocean currents

C. Determining the time around the world

D. Measuring distance on the equator

56. Historians state that the West helped to speed up the Industrial Revolution. Which one of the following was not a reason for this?

A. Food supplies for the ever-increasing urban populations came from farms in the West.

B. A tremendous supply of gold and silver from western mines provided the capital needed to build industries.

C. Descendants of western settlers, educated as engineers, geologists, and metallurgists in the East, returned to the West to mine the mineral resources needed for industry.

D. Iron, copper, and other minerals from western mines were important resources in manufacturing products.

57. In the United States government, the power of taxation and borrowing is

A. Implied or suggested

B. Concurrent or shared

C. Delegated or expressed

D. Reserved

58. **The post-Civil War years were a time of low public morality, a time of greed, graft, and dishonesty. Which one of the reasons listed would not be accurate?**

   A. The war itself because of the money and materials needed to carry on war

   B. The very rapid growth of industry and big business after the war

   C. The personal example set by President Grant

   D. Unscrupulous heads of large impersonal corporations

59. **Studies in astronomy, skills in mapping, and other contributions to geographic knowledge came from**

   A. Galileo

   B. Columbus

   C. Eratosthenes

   D. Ptolemy

60. **Which one of the following would not be considered a result of World War II?**

   A. Economic depressions and slow resumption of trade and financial aid

   B. Western Europe was no longer the center of world power

   C. The beginnings of new power struggles not only in Europe but in Asia as well

   D. Territorial and boundary changes for many nations, especially in Europe

61. **The study of the ways in which different societies around the world deal with the problems of limited resources and unlimited needs and wants is in the area of**

   A. Economics

   B. Sociology

   C. Anthropology

   D. Political science

62. Nineteenth century imperialism by Western European nations had important and far-reaching effects on the colonial peoples they ruled. All four of the following are the results of this. Which one was most important and had lasting effects on key 20th century events?

    A. Local wars were ended

    B. Living standards were raised

    C. Demands for self-government and feelings of nationalism surfaced

    D. Economic developments occurred

63. After the War of 1812, Henry Clay and others proposed economic measures, including raising tariffs to protect American farmers and manufacturers from foreign competition. These measures were proposed in the period known as

    A. Era of Nationalism

    B. American Expansion

    C. Era of Good Feeling

    D. American System

64. "These are the times that try men's souls" were words penned by

    A. Thomas Jefferson

    B. Samuel Adams

    C. Benjamin Franklin

    D. Thomas Paine

65. In countries with more than two political parties, when no one party gains a majority in the legislative body, two or more parties must

    A. Join up to make a majority

    B. Have a run-off election among the top three parties

    C. Arrange with the other parties for another election

    D. Appeal to the highest court for arbitration

66. The Age of Exploration begun in the 1400s was led by

    A. The Portuguese

    B. The Spanish

    C. The English

    D. The Dutch

67. Which one of the following is not a function or responsibility of the U.S. political parties?

    A. Conducting elections or voting process

    B. Obtaining funds needed for election campaigns

    C. Choosing candidates to run for public office

    D. Making voters aware of issues and other public affairs information

68. The economist who disagreed with the idea that free markets lead to full employment and prosperity and suggested that increasing government spending would end depressions was

A. Keynes

B. Malthus

C. Smith

D. Friedman

69. The study of the social behavior of minority groups would be in the area of

A. Anthropology

B. Psychology

C. Sociology

D. Cultural geography

70. An extensive knowledge of surgery and medicine as well as principles of irrigation, fertilization and terrace farming was unique to

A. The Mayas

B. The Atacamas

C. The Incas

D. The Tarapacas

71. The idea of universal peace through world organization was a philosophy of

A. Rousseau

B. Immanuel Kant

C. Montesquieu

D. John Locke

72. Which ancient civilization is credited with being the first to develop irrigation techniques through the use of canals, dikes, and devices for raising water?

A. The Sumerians.

B. The Egyptians

C. The Babylonians

D. The Akkadians

73. The study of past human cultures is

A. History

B. Anthropology

C. Cultural geography

D. Archaeology

74. The "father" of modern economics is considered by most economists today to be

A. Thomas Robert Malthus

B. John Stuart Mill

C. Adam Smith

D. John Maynard Keynes

75. The ideas and innovations of the period of the Renaissance were spread throughout Europe mainly because of

A. Extensive exploration

B. Craft workers and their guilds

C. The invention of the printing press

D. Increased travel and trade

76. The American labor union movement started gaining new momentum

A. During the building of the railroads

B. After 1865 with the growth of cities

C. With the rise of industrial giants such as Carnegie and Vanderbilt

D. During the war years of 1861-1865

77. Soil erosion is most likely to occur in large amounts in

A. Mountain ranges

B. Deserts

C. Tropical rainforests

D. River valleys

78. The father of Switzerland's Protestant Revolution was

A. Calvin

B. Zwingli

C. Munzer

D. Leyden

79. The principle that "men entrusted with power tend to abuse it" is attributed to

A. Locke

B. Rousseau

C. Aristotle

D. Montesquieu

80. After 1783, the largest "land owner" in the Americas was

A. Britain

B. Spain

C. France

D. United States

81. **Any item or service that an industry produces is referred to by economists as**

    A. Output

    B. Enterprise

    C. Arbitrage

    D. Mercantile

82. **After the Civil War, the U.S. adapted an attitude of isolation from foreign affairs. But the turning point marking the beginnings of the U.S. toward becoming a world power was**

    A. World War I

    B. Expansion of business and trade overseas

    C. The Spanish-American War

    D. The building and financing of the Panama Canal

83. **The major responsibility for providing most of the services needed by the people is handled by**

    A. Local governments with federal assistance

    B. State governments with federal assistance

    C. State and local governments

    D. Local governments only

84. **The English explorer who gave England its claim to North America was**

    A. Raleigh

    B. Hawkins

    C. Drake

    D. Cabot

85. **The three-day Battle of Gettysburg was the turning point of the Civil War for the North leading to ultimate victory. The battle in the West reinforcing the North's victory and sealing the South's defeat was the day after Gettysburg at**

    A. Perryville

    B. Vicksburg

    C. Stones River

    D. Shiloh

86. **The study of the exercise of power and political behavior in human society today would be conducted by experts in**

    A. History

    B. Sociology

    C. Political science

    D. Anthropology

87. **Which one of the following Indian groups was not found in the West Indies?**

    A. Totonacs

    B. Caribs

    C. Ciboney

    D. Arawaks

88. **Potential customers for any product or service are not only called consumers but can also be called a**

    A. Resource

    B. Base

    C. Commodity

    D. Market

89. **An early cultural group was so skillful in navigating on the seas that they were able to sail at night guided by stars. They were the**

    A. Greeks

    B. Persians

    C. Minoans

    D. Phoenicians

90. **One method of trade restriction used by some nations is**

    A. Limited treaties

    B. Floating exchange rate

    C. Bill of exchange

    D. Import quotas

91. **A political system in which the laws and traditions put limits on the powers of government is**

    A. Federalism

    B. Constitutionalism

    C. Parliamentary system

    D. Presidential system

92. **Which one of the following did not contribute to the early medieval European civilization?**

    A. The heritage from the classical cultures

    B. The Christian religion

    C. The influence of the German Barbarians

    D. The spread of ideas through trade and commerce

93. **The Roman Empire gave so much to the world, especially the Western world. Of the legacies below, the most influential, effective, and lasting is**

A. The language of Latin

B. Roman law, justice, and political system

C. Engineering and building

D. The writings of its poets and historians

94. **Charlemagne's legacy to Western civilization is seen today in**

A. Separation of church and state

B. Strong military for defense

C. The grand jury system

D. Educational training

95. **Public administration, such as public officials in the areas of budgets, accounting, distribution of public funds, and personnel management, would be a part of the field of**

A. Economics

B. Sociology

C. Law

D. Political science

96. **"Marbury vs Madison (1803)" was an important Supreme Court case which set the precedent for**

A. The elastic clause

B. Judicial review

C. The supreme law of the land

D. Popular sovereignty in the territories

97. **Which one of the following is not a use for a region's wetlands?**

A. Produces fresh clean water

B. Provides habitat for wildlife

C. Provides water for hydroelectric power

D. Controls floods

98. **The philosopher who coined the term "sociology" also stated that social behavior and events could be measured scientifically. He is identified as**

A. Auguste Comte

B. Herbert Spencer

C. Rousseau

D. Kant

99. **The belief that the United States should control all of North America was called**

    A. Westward Expansion

    B. Pan Americanism

    C. Manifest Destiny

    D. Nationalism

100. **A well-known World War II figure who said that democracy was like a rotting corpse that had to be replaced by a superior way of life and more efficient government was**

    A. Hitler

    B. Stalin

    C. Tojo

    D. Mussolini

101. **The Radical Republicans who pushed the harsh Reconstruction measures through Congress after Lincoln's death lost public and moderate Republican support when they went too far**

    A. In their efforts to impeach the President

    B. By dividing ten southern states into military- controlled districts

    C. By making the ten southern states give freed African-Americans the right to vote

    D. Sending carpetbaggers into the South to build up support for Congressional legislation

102. **The economic system promoting individual ownership of land, capital, and businesses with minimal governmental regulations is called**

    A. Macro-economy

    B. Micro-economy

    C. Laissez-faire

    D. Free enterprise

103. A political philosophy favoring or supporting rapid social changes in order to correct social and economic inequalities is called

    A. Nationalism

    B. Liberalism

    C. Conservatism

    D. Federalism

104. China's last imperial ruling dynasty was one of its most stable and successful and, under its rule, Chinese culture made an outstanding impression on Western nations. This dynasty was

    A. Ming

    B. Manchu

    C. Han

    D. Chou

105. Development of a solar calendar, invention of the decimal system, and contributions to the development of geometry and astronomy are all the legacy of

    A. The Babylonians

    B. The Persians

    C. The Sumerians

    D. The Egyptians

106. The study of "spatial relationships and interaction" would be done by people in the field of

    A. Political science

    B. Anthropology

    C. Geography

    D. Sociology

107. The circumference of the earth, which greatly contributed to geographic knowledge, was calculated by

    A. Ptolemy

    B. Eratosthenes

    C. Galileo

    D. Strabo

108. The first European to see Florida and sail along its coast was

    A. Cabot

    B. Columbus

    C. Ponce de Leon

    D. Narvaez

109. Which one of the following events did not occur during the period known as the "Era of Good Feeling"?

   A. President Monroe issued the Monroe Doctrine

   B. Spain ceded Florida to the United States

   C. The building of the National Road

   D. The charter of the second Bank of the United States

110. Florida's first governor after becoming a territory of the United States was

   A. William Henry Harrison

   B. Andrew Jackson

   C. Zachary Taylor

   D. Winfield Scott

111. The world religion which includes a caste system is

   A. Buddhism

   B. Hinduism

   C. Sikhism

   D. Jainism

112. The idea that continued population growth would, in future years, seriously affect a nation's productive capabilities was stated by

   A. Keynes

   B. Mill

   C. Malthus

   D. Friedman

113. After World War II, the United States

   A. Limited its involvement in European affairs

   B. Shifted foreign policy emphasis from Europe to Asia

   C. Passed significant legislation pertaining to aid to farmers and tariffs on imports

   D. Entered the greatest period of economic growth in its history

114. **France decided in 1777 to help the American colonies in their war against Britain. This decision was based on**

    A. The naval victory of John Paul Jones over the British ship "Serapis"

    B. The survival of the terrible winter at Valley Forge

    C. The success of colonial guerilla fighters in the South

    D. The defeat of the British at Saratoga

115. **Tallahassee, Florida's capital, was the only Confederate capital east of the Mississippi River that did not fall into Union hands. The decisive battle that saved Tallahassee was fought at**

    A. St. Marks

    B. Wakulla

    C. Wacissa

    D. Natural Bridge

116. **The British period of control over Florida was characterized by**

    A. The building of Fort Caroline

    B. The settlement of Amelia Island

    C. The division of Florida into two separate colonies of East and West Florida

    D. The setting up of Tallahassee as a meeting place and junction point for both colonies

117. **A number of women worked hard in the first half of the 19th century for women's rights but decisive gains did not come until after 1850. The earliest accomplishments were in**

    A. Medicine

    B. Education

    C. Writing

    D. Temperance

118. **Nineteenth century German unification was the result of the hard work of**

    A. Otto von Bismarck

    B. Kaiser William II

    C. von Moltke

    D. Hindenburg

119. The geographical drought-stricken region of Africa south of the Sahara and extending east and west from Senegal to Somalia is

A. The Kalahari

B. The Namib

C. The Great Rift Valley

D. The Sahel

120. The idea or proposal for more equal division of profits among employers and workers was put forth by

A. Karl Marx

B. Thomas Malthus

C. Adam Smith

D. John Stuart Mill

121. The term that best describes how the Supreme Court can block laws that may be unconstitutional from being enacted is:

A. Jurisprudence

B. Judicial Review

C. Exclusionary Rule

D. Right Of Petition

122. On the spectrum of American politics the label that most accurately describes voters to the "right of center" is:

A. Moderates

B. Liberals

C. Conservatives

D. Socialists

123. Marxism believes which two groups are in continual conflict?

A. Farmers and landowners

B. Kings and the nobility.

C. Workers and owners

D. Structure and superstructure

124. The United States legislature is bi-cameral, this means:

A. It consists of several houses

B. It consists of two houses

C. The Vice-President is in charge of the legislature when in session.

D. It has a upper house and a lower house

125. What Supreme Court ruling established the principal of Judicial Review?

A. Jefferson vs. Madison

B. Lincoln vs. Douglas

C. Marbury vs. Madison

D. Marbury vs. Jefferson

126. To be eligible to be elected President one must:

A. Be a citizen for at least five years

B. Be a citizen for seven years

C. Have been born a citizen

D. Be a naturalized citizen

127. The international organization established to work for world peace at the end of the Second World War is the:

A. League of Nations

B. United Federation of Nations

C. United Nations

D. United World League

128. Which of the following is a example of a direct democracy?

A. Elected representatives

B. Greek city-states

C. The United States Senate

D. The United States house of representatives

129. The political document that was the first to try to organize the newly *independent* American Colonies was the:

A. Declaration of Independence

B. Articles of Confederation

C. The Constitution

D. The Confederate States

130. **The first organized city-states arose in:**

    A. Egypt

    B. China

    C. Sumer

    D. Greece

131. **Which of the three branches of government is responsible for taxation?**

    A. Legislative

    B. Executive

    C. Judicial

    D. Congressional

132. **The founder of the first Communist Party, and the first leader of the Soviet Union was:**

    A. Joseph Stalin

    B. Vladimir Lenin

    C. John Lennon

    D. Karl Marx

133. **The first ten amendments to the Constitution are called:**

    A. Bill of Petition

    B. Petition of Rights

    C. Rights of Man

    D. Bill of Rights

134. **Socialists believe that the government should have a _____ role in the economy:**

    A. Lesser

    B. Greater

    C. Equal with business

    D. Less than business

135. **One difference between *totalitarianism* and *authoritarianism* is that totalitarianism believes in:**

    A. Total control over all aspects of society

    B. Minimum government control

    C. There is no difference

    D. The difference is unknown

136. The constitution is called a "living document" because:

A. It has the ability to change with different times

B. It was created by people

C. It is a static document

D. Excessive reliance on the Constitution will kill it

137. In the feudal system who has the most power?

A. The peasant or serf

B. The noble or lord

C. The worker

D. The merchant

138. The idea that the European powers should stay out of the affairs of the American hemisphere is known as:

A. Containment policy

B. The Eisenhower Doctrine

C. Neo-isolationism

D. The Monroe Doctrine

139. In Marxism another name for the workers is the:

A. Proletariat

B. Peasants

C. Bourgeoisie

D. Protester

140. Fascism first arose in:

A. Austria

B. Germany

C. Italy

D. Russia

141. The Exclusionary Rule prevents:

A. Illegally seized evidence from being used in court

B. Persons from incriminating themselves in court

C. Police from entering a private home for any reason

D. Any evidence however gathered from being used in court if it is objected to by one side in a court case

142. **The idea that "the government is best that governs least" is most closely associated with:**

    A. The Soviet Communist system

    B. The American Free Enterprise system

    C. British Conservatism

    D. Mussolini's Corporate State

143. **In the United States Constitution political parties are:**

    A. Never actually mentioned

    B. Called "a necessary part of the political process".

    C. Most effective if they are only two major ones

    D. Called harmful to the political process

144. **Civil suits deal mostly with, but not totally with:**

    A. Money

    B. Violent crime

    C. The government

    D. Not given

145. **"Common law" refers mostly to:**

    A. The precedents and traditions that have gone before in society so that they become accepted norms

    B. The laws dealing with the "common people"

    C. Law that is written and codified

    D. The House of Commons in Great Britain

146. **Anarchists believe in:**

    A. Strong government

    B. Corporate state system

    C. Weak, mild government

    D. No government

147. The U.S. government's federal system consists of:

A. Three parts, the Executive, the Legislative, and the Judiciary

B. Three parts, the Legislative, the Congress, and the Presidency

C. Four parts, the Executive, the Judiciary, the courts, and the Legislative

D. Two parts, the Government, and the governed

148. One difference between a presidential and a parliamentary system is that in a parliamentary system :

A. The Prime Minister is head of government, while a president or monarch is head of state.

B. The President is head of government, and the Vice-President is head of state

C. The President pro-tempore of the senate is head of state while the prime minister is head of government.

D. The President appoints the head of state

149. The American concept of Manifest Destiny means:

A. America had a right to spread throughout the American continent from coast to coast

B. The United States should respect the right of native peoples it encounters in its push westward

C. The rest of the world powers should stay out of this part of the world

D. America should strive to be the dominant world power

150. In a _indirect_ democracy:

A. All the people together decide on issues

B. People elect representatives to act for them

C. Democracy can never really work

D. Government is less efficient than a direct democracy

151. In a communist system _____ controls the means of production:

   A. A professional managerial class

   B. The owners of business and industry

   C. The workers

   D. The state

152. The Congress can override a presidents veto with a _____ vote:

   A. One-half

   B. Two-thirds

   C. Six-tenths

   D. Three-fourths

153. To become a citizen a individual must generally have lived in the United States for at least:

   A. Six years

   B. Five years

   C. One year

   D. Ten years

154. Give the correct order of the following:

   A. The Constitution, the Declaration of Independence, the Articles of Confederation

   B. The Declaration of Independence, the Constitution, the Articles of Confederation

   C. The Declaration of Independence, the Articles of Confederation, the Constitution

   D. The Articles of Confederation, the Declaration of Independence, the Constitution

155. The ability of the President to veto an act of Congress is an example of:

   A. Separation of Powers

   B. Checks and Balances

   C. Judicial Review

   D. Presidential Perogative

156. **To "impeach" a President means to:**

   A. Bring charges against a president

   B. Remove a president from office

   C. Re-elect the president

   D. Override his veto

157. **An obligation identified with citizenship is:**

   A. Belonging to a political party

   B. Educating oneself

   C. Running for political office

   D. Voting

158. **The doctrine that sought to keep communism from spreading was:**

   A. The Cold War

   B. Roll-back

   C. Containment

   D. Detente

159. **The power to declare war, establish a postal system, and coin money rests with which branch of the government:**

   A. Presidential

   B. Judicial

   C. Legislative

   D. Executive

160. **If a president neither signs nor vetoes a bill officially for ten days it is called:**

   A. A pocket veto

   B. A refused law

   C. Unconstitutional to do that

   D. A presidential veto

161. **What was George Washington's advice to Americans about foreign policy?**

   A. America should have strong alliances

   B. America should avoid alliances

   C. Foreign policy should take precedence over domestic policy

   D. Domestic policy should take precedence over foreign policy

162. **How did the United States gain Florida from Spain?**

A. It was captured from Spain after the Spanish American War

B. It was given to the British and became part of the original thirteen colonies

C. America bought it from Spain

D. America acquired it after the First World War

163. **The belief that Government should stay out of economic affairs is called:**

A. Mercantilism

B. Laissez-faire

C. Democratic-Socialism

D. Corporatism

164. **The term that describes the division of government function is:**

A. Free Enterprise

B. Constitutional Prerogative

C. Checks and Balances

D. Separation of Powers

165. **Which of the following is an important idea expressed in the Declaration of Independence:**

A. People have the right to change their government

B. People should obey the government authority

C. A monarchy is a bad thing

D. Indirect democracy is best

166. **Florida has pioneered what innovative form of local government?**

A. Metropolitan Government

B. Limited government

C. The Mayor-Council system

D. County-Commission system

167. **Machiavelli was most concerned with describing:**

A. Modern warfare

B. Ancient political philosophy

C. Representative government

D. Getting and keeping political power

168. **Oligarchy refers to:**

   A. Rule of a single leader

   B. The rule of a single political party

   C. Rule by a select few

   D. Rule by many

169. **The Judiciary Act of 1789 established the:**

   A. Supreme Court

   B. Principle of Judicial Review

   C. State court system

   D. Federal and circuit court system

170. **The international organization established to work for world peace at the end of the First World War was the:**

   A. United Earth League

   B. Confederate States

   C. United Nation

   D. League of Nations

171. **Which statement closely resembles the political philosophy of John Hobbes?**

   A. Citizens should give unquestioning obedience to the state authority so long as it can maintain public rder

   B. That citizens have a right to rise against the state whenever they choose

   C. All state authority is basically evil and should be eliminated

   D. People are generally good and cooperative if given a chance

172. **As a rule, the relationship between fascism and communism is:**

   A. They are the same thing

   B. Unknown at present

   C. Antagonistic

   D. Cooperative

173. **In the United States the right to declare war is a power of:**

   A. The President

   B. Congress

   C. The Executive

   D. The States

174. To plead "the Fifth Amendment", means to:

A. Refuse to speak so one does not incriminate oneself

B. Plead "no contest" in court

C. Ask for freedom of speech

D. Ask to appear before a judge when charged with a crime

175. A "tort" refers to:

A. A private or civil action brought into court

B. A type of confection

C. A penal offense

D. One who solicits

176. A boycott is:

A. The refusal to buy goods or services

B. A imbalance of trade

C. The refusal to speak in court

D. A Writ of Assistance

177. In the United States checks and balances refers to:

A. The ability of each branch of government to "check", or limit the actions of the others

B. Balance of payments

C. International law

D. The federal deficit

178. An amendment is:

A. A change or addition to the United States Constitution

B. The right of a state to secede from the union

C. To add a state to the union

D. The right of the Supreme Court to check actions of Congress and the President

179. The executive branch refers to:

A. The senate

B. The legislature

C. Congress

D. The President and Vice-President

180. An "Ex Post facto Law" is:

A. A law made against a act after it has been committed

B. A law proclaimed unconstitutional by the Supreme Court

C. An Executive Act

D. A law relating to the postal system

181. The Judiciary refers to:

A. The President

B. Congress

C. The legal system

D. The system of states rights

182. A tariff is:

A. A law passed by the Congress and vetoed by the President

B. A appointed official mandated to preserve public order

C. A tax a government places on internationally traded goods, usually goods entering a country

D. A tax a government places on goods produced for domestic use, another name for it is a "sales tax"

183. Maps as a rule are:

A. All subject to some sort of distortion

B. Always entirely accurate

C. Not very useful in political science studies

D. Difficult usually to understand

184. In a parliamentary system the person who becomes Prime Minister is usually:

A. The leader of the majority party in the legislature

B. Elected by a direct national vote

C. Chosen by the president of the country

D. Chosen by the cabinet

185. The Declaration of Independence owes much to the philosophy of:

A. Vladimir Lenin

B. Karl Marx

C. Thomas Hobbes

D. John Locke

186. **Florida was originally settled by:**

    A. Italy

    B. Great Britain

    C. Spain

    D. France

187. **The "cult of the personality", is an idea most associated with:**

    A. Democracy

    B. Anarchism

    C. Fascism

    D. Communism

188. **The highest appellate court in the United States is the:**

    A. National Appeals Court

    B. Circuit Court

    C. Supreme Court

    D. Court of Appeals

189. **Which political economic system discourages private land ownership?**

    A. Capitalism

    B. Socialism

    C. Agriculturalism

    D. Welfare Capitalism

190. **The Bill of Rights was mostly written by:**

    A. Thomas Jefferson

    B. James Madison

    C. George Washington

    D. Alexander Hamilton

191. **The U.S. Constitution was ratified by the required number of states in:**

    A. August, 1861

    B. July, 1776

    C. June, 1788

    D. September, 1848

192. **To be a *naturalized* citizen means:**

    A. To have been refused citizenship

    B. To have dual-citizenship

    C. To be a "natural", or native born citizen

    D. To acquire citizenship

193. George Washington's opinion of America having trade with other nations was:

   A. Approval in only some instances

   B. Disapproval

   C. Approval

   D. Unsure

194. The "history of all societies is one of class struggle"' is a statement associated with:

   A. John Locke

   B. Thomas Jefferson

   C. Karl Marx

   D. Thomas Hobbes

195. "Walk softly and carry a big stick", is a statement associated with:

   A. Franklin Roosevelt

   B. Theodore Roosevelt

   C. George Washington

   D. Thomas Hobbes

196. Florida has been _____ in local government reform:

   A. A leader

   B. Following

   C. Unsure

   D. Unwilling to change

197. The Bill of rights says that any rights it does not mention are:

   A. Reserved to the federal government

   B. Not important

   C. Judged by the Supreme Court

   D. Reserved to the states or to the people

198. Which political theorist says that capitalism could be maintained if there were sufficient checks on the economy?

   A. Marx

   B. Keynes

   C. Weber

   D. Locke

199. The name for those who make maps is:

A. Haberdasher

B. Geographer

C. Cartographer

D. Demographer

200. An important aspect of statistics is:

A. The rate of proportional increase

B. The rate of increase

C. Tests of redundancy

D. Tests of reliability

201. The process of the state taking over industries and businesses is called:

A. Industrialization

B. Nationalization

C. Redistribution

D. Amalgamation

202. The first permanent settlement in Florida was:

A. St. Marcus

B. Fort Caroline

C. St. Helena

D. St. Augustine

203. The first election in which political parties played a role was in :

A. 1787

B. 1776

C. 1888

D. 1796

204. The vast land area west of the Mississippi River that the United States bought from France was:

A. California and New Mexico

B. The State of Florida

C. The Louisiana Purchase

D. The Gadsen Purchase

205. **The act of hijacking sailors on the high seas was called:**

    A. Internment

    B. Interaction

    C. Interrogation

    D. Impressment

206. **The War of 1812 involved the United States and:**

    A. Russia

    B. Great Britain

    C. France

    D. Spain

207. **The term "*suffrage*", means:**

    A. The right to vote

    B. The power of the court

    C. A Supreme Court ruling

    D. Legislative action

208. **What was "Sewards Folly"?**

    A. The purchase of Alaska

    B. The purchase of Louisiana

    C. The Mexican-American War

    D. The annexation of Texas

209. **Those who wanted the United States to stay out of world affairs were called:**

    A. Neo-Conservatives

    B. Isolationists

    C. Non-Interventionists

    D. Nationalists

210. **The process of putting the features of the earth on a flat surface is called:**

    A. Presentation

    B. Projection

    C. Condensation

    D. Mercatorization

211. **Florida was discovered by:**

    A. Ponce de Leon

    B. Fernando Cortes

    C. Francisco Balboa

    D. Christopher Columbus

212. **The most common type of local government in the United States at present is:**

    A. Commission-Manager

    B. President-Legislature

    C. Council-Manager

    D. Mayor-Council

213. **The first political parties in the United states were:**

    A. Democratic-Republicans and Nationalists

    B. Progressives and Populists

    C. Democratic-Republicans and Federalists

    D. Democrats and Republicans

214. **To become a citizen one must be at least _____ old:**

    A. 25 years

    B. 18 years

    C. 21 years

    D. 19 years

215. **The Spanish-American War started in:**

    A. 1889

    B. 1914

    C. 1927

    D. 1898

216. **A major feature of many multi-party political systems is:**

    A. Separation of powers

    B. Inability to represent sectional interests

    C. Coalition government

    D. Strong centralized government

217. **Which of the following statements about American history is a opinion rather than a fact?**

   A. The doctrine of Manifest Destiny can be said to have been a excuse for the expansionism of the United States on the American continent

   B. Americas wealth, power, and influence increased with its size

   C. Americas expansion was justified by its superior political and economic system

   D. The expansion of the United States was generally detrimental to the interests of native peoples

218. **Which is a shared power of the federal and state governments?**

   A. The power to declare war

   B. The power to build roads

   C. The power to coin money

   D. The power to regulate interstate trade

219. **The foreign policy known as the "Good Neighbor Policy" was associated with the administration of:**

   A. James Madison

   B. Franklin Roosevelt

   C. Woodrow Wilson

   D. Theodore Roosevelt

220. **Direct democracy was a feature of:**

   A. The politics of the Greek city-states

   B. Ancient Rome

   C. Medieval Europe

   D. Sumerian Theocracy

221. **In a Constitutional Monarchy, like that of Great Britain, that has a parliamentary system of government the sovereign takes the place of the:**

   A. Prime Minister

   B. President

   C. Premier

   D. The Speaker of Parliament

222. **In the Federalist Paper 10 what was Madison's main concern?**

    A. Sovereignty

    B. Land reform

    C. Development of small factions which make democracy difficult

    D. Economic instability

223. **The type of city administration that is supposed to eliminate political patronage and fiscal waste is:**

    A. Commission-Council

    B. Mayor-Council

    C. Council-Manager

    D. Metropolitan-Manager

224. **Which of the following statements about the Supreme Court is true?**

    A. "The Supreme Court has only a appellate jurisdiction in all matters".

    B. "The Supreme Court shall have original jurisdiction in all areas involving foreign officials, public officials, and cases in which a state is a party".

    C. "The Supreme Court shall exercise original jurisdiction only over those cases involving the Chief Executive".

    D. "The Supreme Court shall have original jurisdiction over appellate matters only".

225. **"Man was born free and everywhere he is in chains", is a statement associated with:**

    A. Thomas Jefferson

    B. John Locke

    C. Jean-Jacques Rousseau

    D. Karl Marx

226. What happens if the President vetoes a bill?

A. It goes back to Congress which can override the veto with a two thirds vote

B. It goes back to the Congressional committees

C. It goes back to congress which can override it with a three fourths vote

D. It still becomes a law in any case

227. The "Truman Doctrine", was a attempt to prevent the spread of:

A. German expansionism

B. Imperialism

C. Communism

D. Fascism

228. To impeach a president:

A. The charges are brought by the House of Representatives and tried in the Senate

B. The charges are brought by the Senate and tried in the House of Representatives

C. The charges are brought by the states and tried in Congress

D. The charges are brought by Congress and tried before the Supreme Court

229. In the United States the legal voting age is:

A. 19

B. 18

C. 21

D. 25

230. In the United States' electoral system who is allowed to vote in primary elections?

A. Generally, only registered party members are allowed to vote for their candidates in the party

B. Any registered voters may vote for candidates in either party primary

C. Only voters actively engaged in party affairs may vote in a primary

D. Generally, the United States does not engage in primary elections, though they are exceptions.

231. A important *direct* consequence of the First World War was:

A. The end of European colonialism

B. The Great Depression

C. The rise of communism

D. The end of fascism

232. In journalism the term "muckraking", refers to:

A. An attempt to uncover alleged corruption of public officials

B. The attempt to cover up the alleged corruption of public officials

C. The process of buying up various media outlets

D. The investigation of government inefficiency and waste

233. The Voting Rights Act of 1965 sought to:

A. Extend the franchise to minorities

B. Undo the last remaining features of unequal suffrage in the United States

C. Establish the party primary

D. Give the right to vote to women

234. The United States is a:

A. Direct democracy

B. Quasi-democracy

C. Semi-democracy

D. Indirect democracy

235. **The United States is presently comprised of:**

A. 52 states, the District of Columbia, and various overseas territories

B. 48 states, the District of Columbia, and various overseas territories

C. 50 states, the District of Columbia, and various overseas territories

D. 50 states and the District of Columbia only

236. **Powers concurrent to both the federal and state governments are:**

A. To tax, raise a army, to establish courts, to provide for the general welfare, and to fix the standards for weights and measures

B. To tax, to charter banks, to borrow money, to make and enforce laws, and to provide for the general welfare

C. To tax, to borrow money, to establish courts, to regulate international trade, and to make and enforce laws

D. To ratify amendments, to tax, To make and enforce laws, to provide for the general welfare, and to raise a militia

237. **The term "Welfare Capitalism, or Welfare State", is used most often to describe:**

A. The former Soviet Union

B. The interval between Mercantilism and Capitalism

C. The United States and various European countries

D. The Chinese experiments with Communism

238. **A "Poll-Tax", is associated with:**

A. Tariffs on internationally traded goods

B. Voting rights

C. Government construction

D. The income tax structure in a given state

239. **Who of the following wrote about modern economic problems?**

A. John Locke

B. Thomas Hobbes

C. John Maynard Keynes

D. Alexander Hamilton

240. "Gerrymandering" is:

A. The consolidation of various voting districts into larger, more efficient entities

B. The adjustment of voting districts in order to achieve some predetermined goal, usually to try to promote greater minority political representation.

C. The removal of certain inefficient political departments

D. The fixing of the economic infrastructure

241. The Spanish-American war broke out because of Spanish actions in:

A. Florida

B. Haiti

C. Mexico

D. Cuba

ANSWER KEY

1. B	41. B	81. C	121. B	161. B	201. B
2. D	42. A	82. C	122. C	162. C	202. D
3. C	43. B	83. C	123. C	163. B	203. D
4. C	44. A	84. D	124. B	164. D	204. C
5. C	45. C	85. B	125. C	165. A	205. D
6. D	46. A	86. C	126. C	166. A	206. B
7. D	47. B	87. A	127. C	167. D	207. A
8. D	48. A	88. D	128. B	168. C	208. A
9. C	49. C	89. D	129. B	169. D	209. B
10. C	50. A	90. D	130. C	170. D	210. B
11. A	51. A	91. B	131. A	171. A	211. A
12. A	52. B	92. D	132. B	172. C	212. D
13. D	53. B	93. B	133. D	173. B	213. C
14. B	54. D	94. C	134. B	174. A	214. B
15. A	55. C	95. D	135. A	175. A	215. D
16. C	56. C	96. B	136. A	176. A	216. C
17. D	57. B	97. C	137. B	177. A	217. C
18. C	58. C	98. A	138. D	178. A	218. B
19. C	59. D	99. C	139. A	179. D	219. D
20. B	60. A	100. D	140. C	180. A	220. A
21. A	61. A	101. A	141. A	181. C	221. B
22. B	62. C	102. D	142. B	182. C	222. C
23. A	63. D	103. B	143. A	183. A	223. C
24. C	64. D	104. B	144. A	184. D	224. B
25. D	65. A	105. D	145. A	185. D	225. C
26. D	66. A	106. C	146. D	186. C	226. A
27. C	67. A	107. B	147. A	187. C	227. C
28. A	68. A	108. A	148. A	188. C	228. A
29. A	69. C	109. A	149. A	189. B	229. B
30. A	70. C	110. B	150. B	190. B	230. A
31. C	71. B	111. B	151. D	191. C	231. C
32. A	72. A	112. C	152. B	192. D	232. A
33. C	73. D	113. D	153. B	193. C	233. B
34. A	74. C	114. D	154. C	194. C	234. D
35. D	75. C	115. D	155. B	195. B	235. C
36. A	76. D	116. C	156. A	196. A	236. B
37. A	77. C	117. B	157. D	197. D	237. C
38. A	78. B	118. A	158. C	198. B	238. B
39. A	79. D	119. D	159. C	199. C	239. C
40. C	80. B	120. D	160. A	200. D	240. B
					241. D

"What a delightful surprise, I always thought it just trickled down to the poor."

"We've thought and thought, but we're at a loss about what to call ourselves. Any ideas?"

"What's amazing to me is that this late in the game we still have to settle our differences with rocks."

"Mrs. Hammond, I'd know you anywhere from little Billy's portrait of you."

"Are we there yet?"

"Gosh, now we've seen everything!"